Wai Lana's™
FAVORITE
JUICES

Wai Lana's™
FAVORITE
JUICES

WAI LANA PRODUCTIONS
P.O. BOX 6146, MALIBU, CA 90264
WEBSITE: WAILANA.COM
EMAIL: INFO@WAILANA.COM

PRINTED IN HONG KONG

ISBN 0-9725618-5-4

07 06 05 04 03   5 4 3 2 1

Food Photographer: MICHAL NAPIERZYNSKI
Home Economist: JANA GATIEN
Stylists: MICHAL NAPIERZYNSKI AND JANA GATIEN
Lifestyle Photographers: RICHARD LOWTHER,
JOHN BISHOP AND KATIE PRICE
Layout and Design Director: CASSANDRA HOLMES
Graphic Artists: LARRY OLSEN AND KATIE PRICE
Editor: JANA GATIEN
Nutritional Consultant: BRANDON RAYNOR, N.D.

TABLE OF CONTENTS

Dear Friend,

As a mother, vegetarian, and yoga practitioner, the quality of the food I prepare for myself and those I love is naturally very important to me. And since you're reading this book, I know that you also appreciate the connection between the food choices we make and the health we experience.

When I first started juicing a couple of decades ago, I was fasting every Monday and wanted something light but sustaining to drink on those days. So after hearing about the wonders of juicing from a knowledgeable friend, I decided to invest in a good juicer. On my first juice fast, I was amazed by how much energy I had. I was also excited by how completely delicious and satisfying the fresh juices were—I didn't experience any hunger at all. Most importantly, I noticed how easy it was to bend, stretch, and focus while practicing yoga and meditation.

Quality nutrition and self-control are both an essential part of a yoga diet and lifestyle. So whether you're fasting, trying to lose weight, or just getting healthy, a juicing habit can curb your appetite and make a yoga lifestyle easy, energizing, and delicious.

After years of personal research and experimentation, I've put together 88 of my favorite recipes in this book to share with you. Some of these recipes are my favorites and others are my kids' favorites—yes, my kids have been drinking their favorite fresh juices and smoothies since they were little.

It is my sincere hope that this book will inspire you in your effort to improve your own health and the health of those you love by bring everyone in your family nourishment, vitality, and lots of pleasure.

Let's drink to our health!

Wishing you the best,

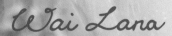

TO YOUR HEALTH

Welcome to the vital world of rejuvenated health.

TO YOUR HEALTH

The first time I tasted fresh carrot juice, I said to myself, "This is truly a gift from heaven!" I was instantly hooked on fresh juices: the straight-from-the-garden taste, the vibrant colors, the genuinely natural smell, and the refreshing burst of energy.

But I did not appreciate how precious this heavenly gift was until I saw my children becoming as hooked as I was on the wonderful taste of fresh juices. As I watched them grow by leaps and bounds, their skin, hair, and teeth strong and healthy, their minds clear and alert, and their appetites for soda pop and junk food practically nonexistent, I was often overwhelmed with feelings of thankfulness. After all, like all mothers, nothing is as important to me as the health of my children.

Naturally, my family and yours fare best—physically, emotionally, and mentally—when our bodies are properly nourished. Proper nourishment also curbs cravings for overly processed, fatty foods that produce low energy, poor health, and ultimately disease.

One of the fastest, easiest ways to replenish vitamins, minerals, and enzymes and undo the damage caused by poor eating habits is to drink the juice of fresh fruits and vegetables. In fact, on an empty stomach, fresh juice can be absorbed into the bloodstream and start renewing your energy within 15 minutes.

REPLENISH, REVITALIZE, AND PROTECT YOUR BODY

Fresh fruits and vegetables provide a wealth of essential vitamins and minerals, especially those that act as antioxidants. Antioxidants like vitamins A, C, and E and selenium help protect our bodies from cell damage caused by overexposure to sunlight, pollutants in the air and water, toxins and additives in our food supply, nicotine, alcohol, and radiation coming from various objects in our environment. All of these factors can slowly chip away at our health and accelerate the aging process. They can also plant seeds for future disease, especially cancer. Antioxidants not only protect your health, but they also rejuvenate your skin, help lower cholesterol, energize your body, and keep your mind alert.

In order to digest our food and absorb vital nutrients like antioxidants, our bodies also need enzymes. Abundant in fresh juices, enzymes are necessary for just about every function in the body. Whether it's digestion, absorption, immune function, or nerve impulse transmission, our bodies could not survive without enzymes.

To increase our chances of living a disease-free, energetic life, the addition of fresh juices to our lifestyle is a tasty, quick, and easy way to start.

CLEANSE AND REGENERATE

Though vegetable juices are very toning and rejuvenating to the body, fruit juices are generally seen as the best cleansers. Removing toxins and cholesterol from the intestines and bloodstream, fruit juices are useful for preventing disease and boosting energy levels. Fruits are also delicious and healthy when blended into a fiber-rich smoothie. Always be sure to dilute fruit juice with water, especially if you have trouble balancing blood sugar.

Alternatively, you can stick with health-building vegetable juices. Vegetable juices are the regenerators of the body, nourishing down to a cellular level. They reduce acidity, thereby soothing irritated skin and easing indigestion. They fortify the blood. They strengthen the organs, glands, nerves, and immune system. Vegetable juices also act as powerful cleansers of the digestive tract and blood.

THE QUICKEST SOURCE OF QUALITY NUTRITION

Everyone's body needs small amounts of different nutrients every day to function properly. These nutrients are meant to come from the food we eat. Although supplements can help, nothing beats the naturally occurring synergy, or harmonious system, of nutrients present in fresh fruits and vegetables.

Nutrition is a delicate system that works best when we have an idea of how it works—and make the right choices.

COLOR YOUR DIET

Since I was a child I've been attracted to naturally colorful foods. But when I discovered how many benefits were synonymous with color, I became even more attracted to vibrant fruits and vegetables like melons, beets, berries, tomatoes, carrots, and greens. For many years I've kept nutrition simple by adhering to one standard: the brighter the food, the better.

Although scientists are just beginning to understand the complex phytochemicals that lend plant foods their distinct pigments, they do know that these colorful nutrients possess amazing powers to protect your health against disease, degeneration, and premature aging. While it's been shown that many vitamins and supplements can help improve and maintain a person's health, it's sheer foolishness to use supplements in place of colorful fruits and vegetables.

Scientists have not "discovered" (and likely never will) all the vitamins, minerals, and other valuable elements naturally present in fresh fruits and vegetables. So the most complete source of vitamins and minerals is the fresh fruits and vegetables themselves—and the best way to get those vitamins and minerals is through juicing.

Carotenoids like lutein, alpha-carotene, and beta-carotene are powerful antioxidants that boost your immune system, preserve your eyesight (by filtering damaging sunrays), beautify your skin, and guard against heart disease. They are also a vegetarian's main source of vitamin A. Ideal sources include carrots, peppers, cantaloupe, mango, papaya, apricots, orange sweet potatoes, pumpkin, broccoli, kale, spinach, and lettuce. Lending color to watermelon, tomato, and red grapefruit, lycopene is another carotenoid that is helpful in preventing certain forms of cancer, especially that of the prostate. Carotenoids can also help lower cholesterol.

Chlorophyll gives plants their deep green color. It also detoxifies and oxygenates your blood and tissues, builds red blood cells, and strengthens your nervous and immune systems. Leafy greens and green grasses are the best sources.

Concentrated in red and purple grapes and berries (as well as in green tea, turmeric, ginger, grapefruit, and walnuts), polyphenols and flavonoids like anthocyanins fight cancer, tumors, heart disease, and osteoporosis. Anthocyanins also beautify your skin and help prevent urinary tract infections.

TAKING YOUR VITAMINS

Vitamins are complex organic compounds that our bodies need for growth, health, reproduction, and the maintenance of every cell and bodily system.

Vitamins can be broken down into two categories: fat-soluble and water-soluble. Fat-soluble vitamins like A, D, E, and K are stored in fat and cannot be absorbed unless there is some fat present in the diet. When juicing, you can always add a teaspoon of flax oil to maximize nutrient absorption. Water-soluble vitamins like the B-complex and vitamin C, on the other hand, pass through the body quickly and should be replenished on a daily basis.

The Complex B-Complex

Deficiency in one B vitamin is rare; people are usually deficient in several of them. If you suspect that you may be deficient, don't supplement with large doses of a single B vitamin without increasing your intake of the other B vitamins.

Vitamin	Function	Symptoms of Deficiency	Best Sources
A Beta-carotene is the plant source of vitamin A, converting to vitamin A once inside the body. Beta-carotene is also known as provitamin A.	Free-radical-fighting antioxidant that protects the immune system, strengthens and repairs bones and tissues, maintains healthy skin, and improves eyesight. Excellent for cancer and all skin and respiratory problems.	Poor night vision. Eye problems. Dry skin. Acne. Poor immune function. Slow growth. Reproductive failure.	Carrots, orange sweet potatoes, red and yellow peppers, squash, apricots, melons, mango, papaya, all dark leafy greens, broccoli, cabbage, seaweed (like arame, dulse, hijiki, kelp, and nori), algae (like spirulina).
B-Complex	A team of coenzymes necessary for maintaining healthy nerves, skin, hair, liver, eyes, mouth, and gastrointestinal muscles. Essential for metabolism. Can be helpful in cases of depression and anxiety.	Depression. Anxiety. Nervousness. Low energy. See the following individual vitamins for more symptoms.	Whole grains (like wheat, brown rice, oats, and rye), nuts, legumes, fruits, vegetables.

Vitamin	Function	Symptoms of Deficiency	Best Sources
Choline	Protects the brain and nerves from damage and degeneration. Helps metabolize fat and regulate the liver and gallbladder. A major component of lecithin.	Fatty liver. Bleeding kidneys. High blood pressure.	Leafy greens, sprouts, legumes (especially garbanzo beans and soybeans).
Inositol	Necessary for fat metabolism and hair growth. Helpful in preventing depression and nervous disorders.	Constipation. Eczema. Hair loss. High cholesterol.	Leafy greens, citrus fruits, cantaloupe, nuts, seeds, grains.
PABA Para- aminobenzoic Acid	Helps protect your skin from sun and wind, minimize wrinkles, and prevent hair loss and premature grayness. Helps form red blood cells. Necessary for protein metabolism.	Fatigue. Irritability. Depression. Nervousness. Constipation. Headache. Digestive disorders.	Root vegetables, dark leafy greens, sprouts, broccoli, wheat (especially wheat germ), oat bran, brown rice.
B_1 Thiamine	Helps keep you mentally alert. Necessary for converting food into energy. Good for the nervous system, heart, and muscles.	Easy fatigability. Indigestion. Irregular heartbeat. Confusion. Constipation. Poor memory. Irritability. Depression.	Wholegrain breads and cereals, brown rice, millet, rye, garlic, nutritional/brewer's yeast, potatoes, cashews, pecans, sunflower seeds, legumes, seaweed.
B_2 Riboflavin	Essential for body growth and repair as well as for energy production and release. Needed for the endocrine glands, nervous system, and healthy eyes.	Low energy. Strained eyesight. Red, itchy eyes. Light sensitivity. Cracks in the corners of the mouth. Inflamed tongue. Dizziness.	Wholegrain breads and cereals, yogurt, fruits, nuts, leafy greens, avocado, cruciferous vegetables (broccoli, cabbage, cauliflower, and brussels sprouts), legumes, nutritional/brewer's yeast.

Vitamin	Function	Symptoms of Deficiency	Best Sources
B$_3$ Niacin	Unlocks energy from food. Helps maintain the nervous system, skin, and gums. Improves circulation and lowers cholesterol. May help prevent skin cancer.	Lack of energy. Insomnia. Depression. Rough skin. Memory loss.	Wholegrain breads and cereals, legumes, peanuts, dairy products, leafy greens, potatoes, figs, prunes, nutritional/brewer's yeast.
B$_5$ Pantothenic Acid	Reduces stress levels. Regulates immune function and supports the adrenal glands. Helps the body retain and use vitamin C. Necessary for the metabolism of food and release of energy. Vital for the formation and function of hormones.	Stress and nervousness. High cholesterol. Headache. Fatigue. Insomnia.	Nutritional/brewer's yeast, broccoli, mushrooms, whole grains, brown rice, legumes, nuts.
B$_6$ Pyridoxine	Essential for metabolism and nervous system and immune function. Regulates serotonin levels in the body. Helpful for circulation, red blood cell production, and relief of PMS symptoms (water retention, irritability).	Anemia. Depression. Irritability. Dry skin disorders. Acne. Cracks around the mouth and eyes. Low blood sugar. Hair loss. Visual disturbances.	Wholegrain breads and cereals, broccoli, spinach, carrots, peas, lentils, avocado, nuts (especially walnuts), rice, sunflower seeds, quinoa, alfalfa, grapes, bananas.
B$_8$ Biotin	Necessary for skin elasticity. Essential for the metabolism of food and release of energy.	Brittle nails. Dry skin. Wrinkles. A grayish complexion. Depression. Hair loss. Sleepiness.	Soy, kidney, and lima beans, dark leafy greens, nuts, mushrooms, barley, avocado, oats, rice bran, legumes, whole wheat, nutritional/brewer's yeast.
B$_9$ Folate, Folic Acid	Necessary for the formation and synthesis of DNA. Also needed for red blood cell production and a healthy nervous system. Protects against heart disease, birth defects, osteoporosis, and cancer. Helps liver and brain function.	Anemia. Depression. Mood changes. Pallor. Weakness. Insomnia. Sores in the corners of the mouth. Poor growth. Forgetfulness. B$_{12}$ deficiency.	Wholegrain breads and cereals, yeast, dark leafy greens, broccoli, asparagus, legumes, seeds.

Vitamin	Function	Symptoms of Deficiency	Best Sources
B$_{12}$ Cyanocobalamin	Necessary for the synthesis of red blood cells, keeping a healthy nervous system, and the proper functioning of all cells, bone marrow, and the intestines. Good for migraine headaches and depression.	Anemia. Fatigue. Depression. Nerve degeneration. Pallor. Sore limbs. Decreased sensory perception.	Nutritional/brewer's yeast, shiitake mushrooms, milk, yogurt, cheese, sourdough bread, tofu, sauerkraut, B$_{12}$-fortified soymilks and cereals.
C Ascorbic Acid	Antioxidant. Builds the immune system and resistance to infection. Necessary for collagen formation and for healthy skin, teeth, and bones. Needed for iron and calcium absorption. Helps prevent high blood pressure and hardening of the arteries. May help promote weight loss and reduce cholesterol. Needed for tissue growth and repair.	Bleeding gums. Loose teeth. Easy bruising. Irritability. Increased susceptibility to illness and infection. Weakness and fatigue. Muscle and joint pain. Slow healing of wounds and bruises. Nosebleeds.	Most fruits and vegetables, especially dark leafy greens, cayenne and bell peppers, tomatoes, cruciferous vegetables, citrus fruits, papaya, cantaloupe, and mustard seeds.

Both vitamins and minerals are generally depleted by stress, caffeine, alcohol, smoking, antibiotics, sleeping pills, junk foods, excessive sugar intake, excessive protein intake, dieting, illness, surgery, extreme heat, radiation, pollution, pain relievers, and the use of laxatives and diuretics.

Vitamin	Function	Symptoms of Deficiency	Best Sources
D	Essential for growth and for healthy bones and teeth. Helps the body use and absorb calcium. Essential during menopause and child growth.	Poor calcium absorption. Softening of the bones. Stunted growth. Bone deformity. Osteoporosis. Weakness. Anemia.	Sunshine, butter, milk, yogurt, vegetable oils.
E **Tocopherol**	Essential for healthy skin and blood circulation. A wonderful antioxidant and anticarcinogen. Protects the body against toxins. Lowers bad cholesterol. May play a vital role in slowing the aging process. Good for PMS.	Anemia. Increased risk of heart disease and stroke. Muscle wasting. Fatigue. Reduced pituitary and adrenal gland function. Liver and kidney damage.	Seeds, nuts, legumes, olives, soy products, cold-pressed vegetable oils (sesame, safflower, sunflower), kiwifruit, tomatoes, peas, butter, spinach, avocado, asparagus, wheat germ, whole grains.
F **Unsaturated Essential Fatty Acids, EFAs, Omega-3 and Omega-6 Fatty Acids**	Maintains function of cell membranes while helping lower cholesterol levels. Essential for healthy skin, joint lubrication, inflammatory conditions, and transmission of nerve impulses. Prevents dry skin and hair loss.	Lowered immune system. Slow healing. Hair loss. Eczema. Behavioral disturbances. High cholesterol. Blood clotting. Eventual damage to liver, kidneys, and heart.	Omega-3: Grapeseed oil, flax oil, oils of grains, avocado, soybeans, raw nuts and seeds (such as walnuts, sesame, and sunflower). Omega-6: All vegetable oils, nuts, seeds, grains.
K **Phylloquinone**	Essential for blood clotting. Important for liver function and control of calcium levels.	Hemorrhages. Nosebleeds. Diarrhea. Miscarriages.	Cruciferous vegetables, dark leafy greens, yogurt, molasses.
P **Bioflavonoids**	Strengthens capillaries. Needed for the proper function of vitamin C. Prevents bruising. Promotes circulation. Stimulates bile production. Reduces pain and swelling.	Bleeding gums. Increased susceptibility to cold, eczema, anemia, and bruising.	Citrus fruits (especially the skin, pulp, and white pith), peppers, grapes, garlic, blue and red berries.
U	Helps heal skin and stomach ulcers.		Cabbage, brussels sprouts, kale.

MINERAL MAGIC

Minerals are inorganic (lifeless) compounds that are nonetheless necessary to sustain life. Although a car runs on gasoline for fuel, it first needs a battery to do even that. Minerals are similar to batteries—they enable our bodies to use fuel. In fact, minerals are needed for the proper functioning of all other nutrients. They also help balance the body systems, strengthen immune function, and keep us mentally alert. Derived mostly from foods grown in quality soil, minerals make up about 4 percent of our body weight. Mineral supplements should be sought only in cases of a known deficiency.

Mineral	Function	Symptoms of Deficiency	Best Sources
Calcium	Strengthens and maintains bones and teeth. Necessary for proper function of the nervous system. Assists blood clotting and fat and protein metabolism. Helps regulate muscle contraction and relaxation, including the heartbeat.	Muscle cramps. Joint pain. Weakness. Low blood sugar. Tooth decay or loss. Extreme or long-term deficiency causes osteoporosis.	Dark leafy greens (especially collard greens and kale), watercress, broccoli, seaweed, dairy products, almonds, figs, dates, apricots, parsley, tofu, beans, peas, sunflower and sesame seeds.
Chromium	Essential for insulin function and regulation. Helps regulate blood sugar and cholesterol. Important for metabolism.	Decreased ability to metabolize sugar, fat, and carbohydrates. Depressed growth. High cholesterol. Deficiencies are often associated with diabetes.	Peanuts, apples, grapes, whole grains, cheese, nutritional/brewer's yeast, mushrooms, spinach, honey, molasses.
Copper	Necessary for healthy blood, blood vessels, bones, skin, and nerves. Also needed for proper skeletal, nervous, cardiovascular, immune, and thyroid function. Aids enzyme function and helps the body use iron and vitamin C.	Anemia. Loss of skin or hair color. Degeneration of the nervous system. Skeletal defects. Reproductive problems.	Brown rice, seaweed, wheat germ, nuts (especially almonds), potatoes, beans, leafy greens.

Mineral	Function	Symptoms of Deficiency	Best Sources
Iodine	Essential for proper thyroid function. Protects against radiation. Helps regulate body temperature, energy production, and metabolism. Needed for healthy hair, skin, and nails.	Enlargement of the thyroid (goiter). Hypothyroidism. Rapid pulse. Heart palpitations. Nervousness.	Seaweed, algae, iodized salt.
Iron	A vital component of hemoglobin, a pigment that transports oxygen throughout the body. Essential for immune and thyroid function, metabolism, and a healthy complexion.	Anemia. Fatigue. Weakened immune system. Pallor. Heart palpitations. Brittle nails. Difficulty breathing and swallowing. Anemia is most common in women in their reproductive years.	Whole grains, dark leafy greens, potatoes, dried figs and prunes, raisins, apricots, tofu, beans, molasses, watermelon, sprouts, pistachios, pumpkin seeds, peanuts.
Magnesium	Vital for healthy nerves, strong bones, muscle contraction (including the heartbeat), and metabolism. Helpful during PMS and menopause.	Weak muscles. Irritability. Irregular heartbeat. Confusion.	Nuts (especially almonds), sunflower and pumpkin seeds, soy products, beans, whole grains, wild rice, wheat germ, bananas, parsley, leafy greens.
Manganese	Important for energy function and bone, blood, and tissue formation. Activates enzymes. Feeds the brain and nervous systems.	Loss of hearing. Ringing in the ears. Dizziness.	Whole grains, brown rice, beans, tofu, wheat germ, leafy greens, seaweed, nuts, seeds.
Molybdenum	Necessary for the metabolism of other minerals and for the formation of urine. Reduces toxicity in the body.	Toxicity. Increased risk of disease.	Legumes.
Phosphorus	Works with calcium to maintain healthy teeth and bones. Needed for kidney and nerve function and metabolism. Necessary for digesting carbohydrates and activating B vitamins.	Decreased appetite. Irregular breathing. Bone loss. Weakness. Fatigue.	Almonds, peanuts, seeds, spinach, asparagus, legumes, oatmeal, bran, sweet potato, yogurt.

Mineral	Function	Symptoms of Deficiency	Best Sources
Potassium	Necessary for water balance, blood pressure regulation, heart and kidney function, pH balance, and nerve impulse transmission. Regulates muscle contractions.	Low blood pressure. Dizziness. Muscle cramps. Fainting spells. Dehydration. Weakness. Acne. Dry skin. Poor reflexes. Increased risk of stroke or heart attack.	Fruits, vegetables, dairy products, sunflower seeds, legumes, leafy greens.
Selenium	Prevents free-radical damage. Produces hormones and helps with proper heart and immune function. Preserves tissue elasticity and youthful skin.	Muscular weakness and discomfort. Loose skin and premature aging.	Avocado, garlic, radish, horseradish, onion, shiitake mushrooms, kidney beans, lentils, oats, wholegrain breads and cereals, Brazil nuts, seaweed, dairy products.
Silicon	A tonic for the skeleton, muscles, skin, and organs. Helpful in preventing wrinkles and stretch marks.	Brittle nails. Dry skin and hair. Weakened tissues. Decreased growth. Deficient bone and tooth structure.	Most vegetables, but especially lettuce and cucumber.

LOCALLY
GROWN

Mineral	Function	Symptoms of Deficiency	Best Sources
Sodium	Helps in nerve impulse transmission. Helps regulate blood pressure and water balance in the body.	Dehydration. Dizziness. Vomiting. Deficiency is unlikely; however, toxicity symptoms are edema, weight gain, and high blood pressure.	Most foods.
Sulfur	Sometimes known as the beauty mineral. Helps keep skin clear and youthful. Helps maintain hair, nails, and blood consistency. Helps prevent cell oxidation. Combats bacterial infection.	Caramelized, thickened blood. Brittle nails. Dry, lackluster skin.	Garlic, watercress, alfalfa, onion, horseradish, cruciferous vegetables, asparagus, figs, nuts, papaya, pineapple, dried apricots.
Zinc	Vital for the immune system, digestion, metabolism, and DNA production. Combats the effects of aging, especially in the skin. Plays a key role in hormone production and synthesis.	Stretch marks. White spots on fingernails. Brittle hair and nails. Irregular menstruation. Loss of sense of taste. Weakened immune system. Skin problems. Fatigue. Diarrhea. Infection.	Nuts (especially cashews), pumpkin seeds, wholegrain breads and cereals, legumes (especially lentils), wheat germ, dairy products.

SELECTING THE BEST FRUITS & VEGETABLES

Whether you're dealing with organic or nonorganic fruits and vegetables, always wash them with a diluted nontoxic, biodegradable soap solution or a commercially available nontoxic fruit-vegetable wash. Be sure to rinse them thoroughly with clean drinking water. To be extra careful, you can also add a few drops of grapefruit seed extract to a bowl of water, then soak produce for several minutes. This helps kill parasites and harmful bacteria.

Here are a few more pointers to minimize your exposure to harmful bacteria and toxins:

• Thoroughly wash your hands before preparing any food.
• Wash your sink and all countertops thoroughly when washing and cutting produce.
• Buy fresh-looking fruits and vegetables. Avoid packaged vegetables that smell bad or appear slimy.
• Keep ripe fruits and vegetables in your crisper. Also, cover and refrigerate all cut fruit and vegetables promptly.
• Discard old produce and cut or open fruits and vegetables that have been out of the refrigerator for more than four hours.

STORING YOUR JUICE

Fresh juice tastes best right after it's made. As soon as juice is extracted from the fruit or plant, its nutrients are exposed to oxygen. Once exposed, the enzymes and nutrients gradually oxidize (break down). It's ideal to drink your juice while the enzymes and nutrients are fresh and ready to energize, nourish, and cleanse your body.

For those times when you won't be drinking your juice immediately, here are some suggestions:

• Store the juice in an airtight glass container at a cold temperature (less than 37°F or 3°C).
• Refrigerate your container before you fill it with juice.
• Fill the container to the top to minimize the oxidizing presence of air.
• Drink the juice within 24 hours.

If you are on the go and want to take your juice with you, a good-quality stainless steel or glass thermos is ideal for storage. Not all thermoses are the same, so invest in one with good insulation. Cool the thermos in the refrigerator or freezer before you fill it with juice. This will help keep the juice fresher longer.

BOOST YOUR JUICE

Enhance the healing, energizing, and nourishing powers of fresh
juices with these easy-to-find supplements and herbs.

BOOST YOUR JUICE

Although fresh juices are an abundant source of energy on their own, I never hesitate to add one (or two) of these natural supplements, especially when I'm replacing breakfast or lunch with a juice or smoothie.

Aloe Vera Juice

Aloe vera juice is an ancient tonic for digestive problems like acid stomach, indigestion, constipation, ulcers, and colitis. It is also beautifying and soothing for the skin. Aloe is rich in vitamins A, B-complex, and E, calcium, zinc, protein, enzymes, immune-boosting polysaccharides, and anti-inflammatory and antimicrobial agents. It is cooling by nature and helps protect your body against radiation. Applied externally, aloe vera juice is my favorite remedy for sunburn.

Apple Cider Vinegar

Apple cider vinegar is a popular and inexpensive folk remedy that has been used to treat arthritis, sore throats, bladder infections, prostate disorders, high blood pressure, menstrual disorders, and poor digestion. It also promotes weight loss and helps relieve water retention. Warming and energizing, cider vinegar improves circulation and chi (energy flow) within the body. It is even believed to be a good mood food. I'm always sure to buy raw, unpasteurized apple cider vinegar to ensure that valuable nutrients like enzymes and potassium are still present.

Bee Pollen

Egyptians used it to preserve youth and beauty, Greek Olympians used it to increase energy and endurance—even ancient scriptures like the Bible and the Koran praise the healing and rejuvenating properties of bee pollen. This golden, sweet supplement helps improve overall health, prevent disease, balance metabolism, and boost the immune system. It can even help reduce the symptoms of hay fever and allergies.

Bee pollen contains vitamins A, B-complex, C, D, and E, natural antibiotics, protein (up to 35 percent by weight), enzymes and coenzymes, sterols (plant hormones), essential fatty acids, and an abundance of minerals and trace elements.

Note: Because bee pollen is made from flowers, a small percentage of people may experience an allergic reaction to it. For this reason, it's best to start out with just a few grains and then gradually increase your dosage if you don't experience any reaction.

Flaxseeds and Flax Oil

An excellent source of vitamin A and lecithin, omega-3-rich flaxseeds provide the kind of fat your body needs in order to burn fat. Flaxseeds can also satisfy your body's cravings for fat while stoking your metabolism. For this reason, some health specialists have dubbed flax oil the "nonfat fat." Omega-3 essential fatty acids (EFAs) are major components of nerve cells, cell membranes, and hormonelike substances called prostaglandins, which help regulate every cell, organ, and system in your body and protect it from disease.

The omega-3 fatty acids found in flaxseeds can help lower cholesterol, prevent heart attack and stroke, lower blood pressure, and ease arthritis as well as nourish and beautify your skin. They also help your body to better absorb nutrients. Take 1-2 tablespoons of ground flaxseeds or flax oil daily. Be sure to refrigerate all flax products.

Green Grasses

Providing a rich supply of vital nutrients, green grasses like wheat and barley grass make wonderful sources of nutrition. Ideally these grasses should be juiced fresh, but because most grasses require a special juicer, it's not always possible to make this juice yourself. In the absence of fresh grass juice, green grass powders are still a good source of nutrition. Many companies dry green juices in a way that preserves the enzyme and nutrient content.

Whether fresh or powdered, adding green grasses to your juice or smoothie provides a wealth of vitamins (including folate and B_{12}), beta-carotene (provitamin A), essential fatty acids, lecithin, chlorophyll, protein, phytochemicals, antioxidants, enzymes, minerals, and trace elements. These nutrients help slow cell degeneration and aging as well as protect us from environmental toxins, radiation, and disease-causing carcinogens. Green grasses also help reduce inflammation and heal conditions like asthma, anemia, arthritis, diabetes, cancer, ulcers, chronic fatigue, pancreas, liver, and kidney problems, and many more.

Soy Protein

A good source of protein, this common supplement is ideal for making a smoothie into a meal. Filling and tasty (some brands come in flavors like strawberry shortcake and cappuccino), soy protein powders can make your smoothies taste more like milkshakes. Always look for a brand of soy protein that's free from genetically modified ingredients (GMO-free). If you are sensitive to sweet juices, try adding a scoop of soy protein to minimize the juice's effect on your blood sugar level.

Spirulina

Cooling spirulina provides a wealth of nutrients that are easily absorbed by the body. Both nourishing and cleansing, spirulina helps strengthen and purify the blood, regulate blood sugar levels, and detoxify the kidneys and liver. It promotes good digestion and improves brain function. It also boosts the immune system, fights yeast overgrowth, and helps keep your skin toned, youthful, and blemish-free. Between 60 and 70 percent protein by weight, spirulina is also an outstanding source of beta-carotene (provitamin A), iron, essential fatty acids, B-complex vitamins, chlorophyll, minerals, and trace elements. Spirulina can help curb food cravings, making it a perfect supplement for dieters. It's also beneficial for people with arthritis, acne, anemia, hypoglycemia, and diabetes.

Whey Protein

Whey protein powder is my favorite boost when replacing meals with juices and smoothies. It's low in fat, highly digestible, and blends well with just about any fruit combination. Whey protein is a good source of energy and, like other concentrated proteins, helps the body repair and rebuild tissue. It's about 1 percent lactose and is generally well tolerated even by the lactose-intolerant.

OTHER ADDITIONS

Milk

It's quite easy nowadays to find a type of milk that's tailored to your body's needs. I've used the word "milk" in the following juice recipes as an umbrella term that covers dairy milk, soymilk, rice milk, oat milk, and almond and other nut milks; use whichever one best suits your body—and your taste buds. If you're lactose-intolerant, many reliable dairy alternatives are now fortified with essential nutrients like vitamin B_{12}, calcium, and iron—all of which are abundant in dairy. Many nondairy milks are also excellent sources of protein and come in delicious flavors like vanilla, chocolate, and carob. Because it's thicker and creamier, I don't use coconut milk interchangeably with the other milk varieties. Recipes using coconut milk will call for it specifically.

Soaked Dried Fruits and Nuts

Some of my recipes call for soaked dried fruits and nuts. Soaking them first improves their juiceability and blendability—it even makes nuts more nutritious and digestible.

Soak dried fruits or raw nuts for a minimum of 2 hours in warm water. If you can wait longer, however, soak them overnight in the refrigerator. They will expand considerably, so make sure there's enough water. Two cups of water per 1 cup of fruit or nuts should be adequate. They can soak for up to 2 days.

Spices and Fresh Herbs

I also like to boost juices and smoothies with fresh herbs from the garden or warm winter spices. The juicing of fresh herbs allows us to use the healing system created by nature. Fresh herbs have potent medicinal qualities that help heal and balance our bodies. They can also prevent and relieve conditions ranging from indigestion and arthritis to diabetes and heart disease. They can even help prevent the formation of cancer. On a subtler level, fresh herbs have therapeutic effects on both your mind and body. Some are mellowing, others arousing. Some cool the body, while others have a gentle warming effect. Mix herb juices with other juices, or drink them on their own, diluted with water (1 ounce of herb juice per 8 ounces of water).

SPICES AND FRESH HERBS

Basil
In China, basil is called luole and is considered to have many medicinal properties. Basil helps relieve nausea, indigestion, and stomach cramping. It improves circulation and aids digestion (in fact, Italians have long coupled it with pasta and bread, believing it promotes the digestion of starches). Basil is a gentle relaxant and can even help relieve some headaches and clear the mind.

Cayenne
Though we usually use cayenne to spice up our food, this fiery pepper has much more to offer than just heat. For thousands of years cayenne has been used by experienced herbalists for its diverse healing properties. It aids digestion, improves circulation, helps lower blood pressure and cholesterol, and wards off colds, sinus infections, and sore throats. It also helps reduce fatigue, stimulate metabolism, and ease arthritis. Extremely rich in provitamin A and vitamin C as well as other antioxidants, cayenne gives a tremendous boost to your immune system. It goes well in both fruit and vegetable juices.

Cilantro
This cooling herb is my summer favorite. Cilantro, also known as Chinese parsley or coriander, helps reduce heat in the body and aids the digestive system by stimulating the secretion of digestive juices. Cilantro also reduces gas.

Cinnamon
Cinnamon has natural antifungal and antiviral properties. It helps to alleviate cold and flu symptoms like fever, chills, and cough. It also helps to relieve menstrual cramps and stimulates digestion. Cinnamon possesses hypoglycemic qualities, making it a wonderful food for people with diabetes.

Cumin
Cumin is an Ayurvedic spice that helps digestion by minimizing gas in the stomach and intestines. Cumin ignites the gastric fire without overheating the body. It's good for relieving menstrual and muscle cramps. It's also a mild diuretic.

Dill
A natural digestive aid, this fine herb helps ease cramps, gas, bloating, and upset stomachs. Dill alkalizes the body and helps stabilize blood sugar levels. Dill is also a folk remedy for the hiccups.

Garlic

The healing powers of garlic are truly amazing. Used in many cultures for thousands of years, this natural medicine inhibits viruses, fungi, yeast, parasites, and other harmful microorganisms. It fights cancer and tumor growth, improves circulation, and helps replenish healthy bacteria in the digestive tract. Garlic also helps clear the lungs, restore energy to the body, lower cholesterol, and fight heart disease. When juicing garlic, keep in mind that a little bit goes a long, long way.

Ginger

My favorite spice in cooking is also my favorite to juice with. Used in both Ayurvedic and Chinese medicine for thousands of years, ginger is heating, cleansing, and rejuvenating to your body. Besides lending zest, vitality, warmth, and energy to fruit and vegetable juices alike, ginger helps conditions like asthma, cough, cold, congestion, flu, high cholesterol, water retention, nausea, irregular or painful menstruation, constipation, and poor circulation. Ginger also strengthens your digestive fire, boosts your immune system, and breaks down uric acid in the body.

Mint

Although cooling and calming, mint is actually a mild stimulant. If your body is sensitive, it's wise to avoid using mint before bedtime. Mint is an internal refresher and helps reduce odors in the colon and stomach, improving your breath and body odor. It minimizes gas and helps digestion. Mint also benefits the liver and gallbladder and helps treat cold, flu, and allergy symptoms.

Rosemary

My garden wouldn't be complete without rosemary. Hardy and versatile, rosemary is a great medicinal herb that grows robustly in almost any climate. Rosemary stimulates the heart and circulation as well as bile production in the liver, making it helpful for digestion and elimination. Rich in antioxidants and chlorophyll, rosemary possesses antiseptic properties that combat bacteria and viruses in the body. It can also calm an upset stomach and soothe joint inflammation and headaches. Because it acts as a preservative, some herbalists believe rosemary helps prevent premature aging. Considered an emotionally uplifting herb, rosemary wakes you up and promotes mental clarity and memory function. Caution: Don't use rosemary when pregnant or nursing.

Thyme

A disinfectant for the lungs, thyme is especially helpful in relieving respiratory conditions like asthma and bronchitis. Thyme also helps the body digest fat and relieves gastrointestinal problems like gas and indigestion. Because it has antispasmodic properties, thyme can help alleviate menstrual cramps.

Note: If you have a garden, why not experiment with other common herbs like calming lemon balm, cleansing chives, or a digestive like tarragon? Just a few leaves can infuse your juice with flavor and different healing properties.

FRUIT JUICES

Cleanse, rejuvenate, and energize your body.

FRUIT JUICES

Wonderfully delicious, energizing, and cleansing, most of the fruit recipes in this chapter can either be juiced or blended, depending on how much fiber you'd like. I always recommend diluting fruit juice up to half water, especially if you are juicing for children or people with frail health. If you are juicing for people with diabetes, hypoglycemia, or other blood sugar irregularities, try sticking with more savory recipes like those found in the vegetable juice chapter.

Radiant Beauty

This fruit combination works beautifully together. Not only does it taste delicious, but these ingredients also have a marvelous effect on your nervous system, your digestive system, and especially your skin.

2 CUPS PAPAYA
¼ CUCUMBER
5 FRESH MINT LEAVES
¼ LIME

Blend with:

1 TSP. HONEY
1 GENEROUS TBSP. AVOCADO

Boost

Ancient Egyptians would probably have added a teaspoon of bee pollen to further enhance the beautifying powers of this recipe. I do too occasionally.

Benefits

Thanks to its silicon and potassium content, cucumber rejuvenates your appearance by promoting skin elasticity and reducing blemishes. Cucumber also soothes your nerves and acts as a natural diuretic. The beta-carotene in papaya and the vitamin E in avocado fight free radicals and help prevent premature aging.

Tip

Freeze some chunks of papaya the night before and use them as edible ice cubes.

Tropical Ambrosia

This heavenly blend will fill you up and energize you for hours. As a longtime vegetarian, I often use bee pollen, which provides protein, vitamin B_{12}, lecithin, and nearly all the nutrients needed to sustain life. A boon for your heart, brain, and immune system, this recipe makes a first-rate breakfast.

1 CUP MANGO
1 CUP PINEAPPLE

Blend with:
1 FROZEN BANANA
½ CUP COCONUT MILK
½ CUP WATER
1 TSP. BEE POLLEN

INSTEAD OF COCONUT MILK AND WATER, YOU CAN MAKE THIS RECIPE WITH 1 CUP OF FRESH COCONUT WATER.

Benefits

Though not usually convenient, fresh coconut milk is tastier and far more nutritious than its canned counterpart. A superb source of energy for athletes, fresh-made coconut milk contains a perfect balance of electrolytes (potassium, calcium, magnesium, sodium, and chloride). Electrolytes are necessary for nerve transmission and muscle contraction. They also prevent dehydration. In one of nature's contradictions, coconut is rich in fat yet promotes weight loss.

Tip

Whenever I'm in a tropical location, I like to make my own fresh coconut milk. Simply open a young coconut and drain the water into a cup. Split the coconut in half and spoon out the soft flesh. Blend the coconut water and flesh in a blender until smooth.

Red Raspberry Zinger

Gentle and infused with the calming aroma of basil, this elegant, unique blend is good for easing migraines and anxiety.

⅓ CUP RASPBERRIES
3 PEARS
5 FRESH BASIL LEAVES
½ CUP SPARKLING WATER (ADD AFTERWARD)

Benefits

Basil soothes the nervous system, helping alleviate headaches, fatigue, and depression. Pear juice helps clean the body of toxins by stimulating digestion and elimination. Both raspberries and pears cleanse the urinary tract. Raspberries also help reduce acne and soften rough skin.

Sweet Ginger

My kids call me the Ginger Queen because I'm likely to put ginger in most anything. Besides adding spirit and flavor, ginger helps stimulate metabolism and promote weight loss. Ginger also improves circulation and boosts immunity.

1-INCH PIECE OF FRESH GINGER
2 CUPS PINEAPPLE
2 PLUMS

Benefits

Warming ginger improves circulation by dilating arteries and helping lower cholesterol. With pineapple and plum, this juice supports your lungs and can help relieve coughs, congestion, and even asthma. Ginger ignites your digestive fire, while enzymes in pineapple help your body absorb nutrients.

Tip

Make sure your pineapple is ripe. If you're not sure by looking at it, taste it. If it's more acidic than sweet, it's not ripe. The acids in unripe pineapple can damage your teeth and burn your mouth.

Moving Day

Poor eating habits, stress, and dehydration are common causes of constipation. Try drinking this pleasant fruit fusion every few days for regularity.

2 CUPS PAPAYA
2 PEARS
1-INCH PIECE OF FRESH GINGER

Boost

Enhance the power of this juice by blending it with a teaspoon of flax oil and two soaked prunes. Make it a smoothie by blending with a banana.

Benefits

An excellent source of fiber, papaya has a cleansing and laxative effect on the colon. Papain, an enzyme found in papaya, also fights parasites and harmful bacteria in your digestive tract. Pear is a rich source of pectin, which absorbs toxins in the intestines and stimulates bowel movement. Pear also helps relieve indigestion. Ginger stimulates your digestive juices and can relieve heartburn and nausea.

Berry Mango Bliss

I love any recipe with mango in it. Bursting with colorful nutrition, this light blend has long been a neighborhood favorite. It's absolutely delicious and hits the spot when the kids are hungry for a milkshake. Use regular or frozen fruit.

Blend:
¼ CUP BLUEBERRIES
1½ CUPS MANGO
2 KIWIFRUIT, SKIN REMOVED
⅓ CUP WATER OR MILK

Boost
Try adding a scoop of protein powder.

Benefits

Pureed mango pulp is an excellent intestinal cleanser, absorbing toxins as it moves through the digestive tract. Similarly, blueberries form a gel-like substance that also makes an excellent internal cleanser. Full of enzymes, mango energizes and rehydrates your body, while blueberries provide potent antioxidants. Kiwifruit contain more vitamin C than citrus fruit and provide extra immune support.

Citrus Sunrise

This recipe was my younger daughter's solution to sour grapefruit, and it's become a regular breakfast favorite in our home. Since it strengthens your tissues, arteries, gums, and teeth, this juice is especially helpful for maintaining oral hygiene.

2 PINK GRAPEFRUIT
2 TANGERINES
2 PERSIMMONS

Benefits

This refreshing combination cools and replenishes fluids in the body, making it an ideal drink after your morning workout. It also helps relieve arthritis, acne, and varicose veins. Citrus fruits give a boost to your immune system and help relieve coughs and sore throats. Persimmons help treat gingivitis and canker sores.

Tip

I'm happy to see persimmons, which are common in Asian markets, turning up more and more in regular grocery stores. Always make sure that your persimmons are ripe; otherwise you could be in for an unpleasant surprise! Persimmons are virtually inedible unripe because they're highly astringent. But if unripe persimmons are all you have, you'll be glad to know that they ripen quickly after being frozen briefly, then thawed.

Melon Magic

While many people hesitate to combine quick-digesting melon with other foods, I find melons and berries a harmless and tasty combination. This cooling juice is excellent for relieving both dehydration and fluid retention.

1½ CUPS CANTALOUPE
1½ CUPS HONEYDEW
4 STRAWBERRIES

Boost

Supplement flavor and nutrition with some fresh ginger.

Benefits

Cooling and calming, melons are powerful diuretics that cleanse the kidneys and bladder by flushing excess fluids, waste, and uric acid from the body. This makes melons perfect for juice fasting and weight loss. Compared to other fruit juices, melon juice is relatively low in sugar and full of digestive enzymes. It is also a mild laxative.

Pink Lemonade

I love this sweet summery lemonade not only because it's fresh and thirst-quenching, but also because of its many nutritional benefits. Besides protecting your skin, it also promotes weight loss, boosts your immune system, and helps lower blood pressure.

1 LEMON (INCLUDING A SLIVER OF RIND)
1 CUP STRAWBERRIES
1½ CUPS GREEN GRAPES
½ CUP WATER (REGULAR OR SPARKLING)
(ADD AFTERWARD)

Benefits

Antioxidants, especially the limonene found in lemon rind, help keep your skin clear, vibrant, and protected from skin cancer. Lemon juice stimulates bile production and the elimination of stale bile, enhancing digestion and liver function. This juice also works to strengthen your heart, blood, and circulation.

Aloha Energy

Mouth-watering pineapple and papaya always put me in a tropical mood. They also provide unique digestive enzymes that help our bodies break down and absorb nutrients.

1½ CUPS PINEAPPLE
1½ CUPS PAPAYA
½ CUP COCONUT MILK (ADD AFTERWARD)

Boost

You can make this juice a super-smoothie by blending it with a teaspoon of spirulina and a banana.

Benefits

Rich in powerful enzymes and energy-boosting natural sugars, this juice is a wonderful way to begin your day. Bromelain, a powerful enzyme in pineapple, dissolves mucus, fights bacteria, and soothes inflammation. It can even ease menstrual cramps. Both bromelain and the papain in papaya actively aid protein digestion.

Cottage Cooler

This summertime favorite is always a hit with our guests. Made with fresh stalks from the rhubarb patch in our backyard, it's an excellent juice for all aspects of oral hygiene.

6 STRAWBERRIES
8 INCHES RHUBARB STALK
3 APPLES

Boost

If you like it creamy, blend with ½ cup milk and a frozen banana.

Benefits

Strawberry juice helps relieve gingivitis, while rhubarb juice helps dissolve dental plaque and tartar and correct tooth discoloration. For best effect, swish this juice around in your mouth before swallowing. Rhubarb juice is also an effective laxative.

Caution

Because it is very concentrated in oxalic acid, drinking rhubarb juice too often could damage tooth enamel. Excess or frequent consumption can also increase your risk of kidney stones.

Singer's Cider

Whenever I'm recording music and using my voice a lot, this is my preferred juice to take to the studio. Unique nutrients in this combination provide protection and relief to a sensitive or sore throat. A helpful juice for weight loss, Singer's Cider is also delicious served warm.

1½ CUPS PINEAPPLE
2 PEARS
¼ LEMON
1-INCH PIECE OF FRESH GINGER
1 PINCH CAYENNE PEPPER

Boost

Blend with two soaked dried figs for extra help in relieving a cough.

Benefits

This cider is very helpful in soothing sore throats, persistent coughs, and lung congestion. It helps balance alkaline/acid levels, cleanse the blood and intestines, and destroy viruses, bacteria, and intestinal microbes and parasites. It also stimulates digestion and metabolism.

Kiwi Surprise

Every time I make this luscious blend for my kids, I end up having to make seconds, and sometimes thirds. Light but filling, this fruit fusion is the perfect summer snack.

Blend:
2 KIWIFRUIT, SKIN REMOVED
⅓ CUP RASPBERRIES (FRESH OR FROZEN)
1 BANANA
¾ CUP WATER OR MILK

Boost
Add more fiber and antioxidant protection by including a tablespoon of whole or ground flaxseeds.

Benefits
Along with raspberries, kiwifruit are an excellent source of vitamins C and E, making this combination helpful in preventing oxidative damage—a major cause of cancer, heart disease, and premature aging. Kiwifruit also help rid your body of excess sodium, while raspberries help relieve water retention.

Papaya Paradise

Get out your blender and bring the king and queen of fruits together! Rich in antioxidants and digestive enzymes, this is one of my breakfast favorites, especially with a squeeze of fresh lime.

Blend:

1 CUP PAPAYA
1 CUP MANGO
¼ CUP BLUEBERRIES
½ CUP WATER OR MILK

Boost

You can make this blend a meal by adding a frozen banana and a teaspoon of bee pollen.

Benefits

The fiber and enzymes in this light smoothie make it a fine digestive aid and laxative. These antioxidant-rich fruits also beautify your skin and boost the immune system. Papaya tones the stomach, relieves indigestion, and can even help alleviate arthritic pain.

Fountain of Youth

These beautiful fruits are magic for your complexion. Containing more carotene, or vitamin A, than any other fruit, apricots help tighten your skin and guard against premature aging.

3 APRICOTS (OR 6 DRIED APRICOTS, SOAKED)
2 CUPS PINEAPPLE
4 STRAWBERRIES

Boost

For extra nutrition and flavor, add some fresh ginger.

Benefits

Rich in anti-aging properties, this juice helps firm your skin and give it a healthy carotene glow. To help reduce acne and skin irritations, drink this juice regularly. Both pineapple and strawberries contain natural muscle relaxants and can help relieve sore muscles, menstrual cramps, and arthritic pain.

Carrot Cake Cooler

Energizing, refreshing, and bursting with nutrients, this delightful drink tastes just like carrot cake—without all the fat or calories. If you miss the icing on the cake, simply add a swirl of creamy vanilla soymilk.

2 CARROTS
2 APPLES
1 CUP PINEAPPLE
1-INCH PIECE OF FRESH GINGER
1 PINCH CINNAMON, GROUND CARDAMOM,
   AND/OR PUMPKIN PIE SPICE

Boost

Make this recipe a smoothie by adding a frozen banana, ½ cup milk, and a scoop of protein powder.

Benefits

This juice provides an abundance of enzymes and digestive spices, making it a boon for your digestive system. If taken regularly, these spices keep your digestive fire strong and improve nutrient absorption. Beneficial to your throat and lungs, this hearty, nourishing juice can also be lightly heated.

Raspberry Cream Pie

If you and your family have a sweet tooth, this decadent blend will satisfy it. Tasting as good as it looks, this recipe is also an excellent tonic for cleansing, detoxification, and cancer prevention.

JUICE OF 3 APPLES

Blend with:
⅓ CUP RASPBERRIES
1 FROZEN BANANA
⅓ CUP WATER OR ½ CUP MILK
RASPBERRIES & WHIPPED CREAM FOR GARNISHING

Boost
I sometimes add a teaspoon of apple cider vinegar and/or a scoop of protein powder.

Benefits
Rich in phenols (highly active anticarcinogens), raspberries help destroy free radicals and eliminate toxins from the bloodstream. Like most berries, they help beautify your skin and cleanse the urinary tract. Banana, an excellent strength-building food, coats the digestive tract and soothes indigestion. Apples stimulate digestion and dissolve toxins in the colon.

Mango Berry Fusion

Each time I drink this luscious blend I wish I could give it to those who don't believe that health and great taste can go hand in hand. Fresh and bursting with enzymes and antioxidants, this recipe is a perfect fusion of nutrition and taste.

Blend:
1½ CUPS MANGO
⅓ CUP RASPBERRIES (FRESH OR FROZEN)
1 TBSP. LIME JUICE
½ CUP WATER OR MILK

Benefits
Raspberries help neutralize toxins in your blood and improve the appearance of your skin. Mango, a good source of beta-carotene, also promotes a youthful, vibrant complexion. Its wealth of fiber cleanses the intestines by absorbing toxins and carrying them out of your body.

Tip
To help mangoes ripen more quickly, put them in a paper bag overnight. To speed the process, put some bananas in the sack as well.

Autumn Breeze

Gentle and delicious, fennel lends aromatic flare to simple apple-pear juice. Helpful for regulating your digestive tract and alleviating constipation, this recipe is especially nice in the fall when ingredients are fresh-picked and abundant.

2 APPLES
2 PEARS
1 CUP FENNEL

Boost

For more fiber, you can add a teaspoon of ground flaxseeds.

Benefits

Pectin, a carbohydrate found in both pears and apples, forms a gel in the intestines and absorbs toxins as it moves through. Pectin also removes cholesterol and toxic metals like mercury and lead from the body. Fennel soothes your nerves and can help relieve gas and headaches.

Blackberry Blend

If a picture is worth a thousand words, I don't need to tell you how delicious this gorgeous drink is. Not too sweet, this light blend is perfect for those who want fiber without too much bulk. These antioxidant-rich fruits fight heart disease, skin conditions, and certain forms of cancer, especially prostate cancer.

JUICE OF 2 PINK GRAPEFRUIT

Blend with:

⅓ CUP BLACKBERRIES (FRESH OR FROZEN)
1 FROZEN BANANA
⅓ CUP WATER

Boost

If you'd like to make this a meal, add a scoop of protein powder and a teaspoon of maple syrup.

Benefits

Helpful in lowering cholesterol and preventing it from oxidizing (hardening) in your arteries, this blend is a good friend to your heart. These fruits help keep not only your complexion clear and vibrant, but also your brain. In fact, the antioxidants in this recipe help prevent oxidative damage to the brain, promoting good memory and keen mental function.

Tip

I always include some white grapefruit pith for extra vitamin C and bioflavonoids, which are most concentrated there. You'll find it easier to hand-squeeze the grapefruit because then you won't have to clean your juicer. If you like the visual effect, blend the fruits individually, then layer them.

Cherry Crush

When cherry season begins, don't forget to introduce them to your juicer. Both cherries and oranges strengthen your chi, or life energy. Cherries especially help relieve arthritis, gout, and anemia.

½ CUP PITTED CHERRIES (FRESH OR FROZEN)
3 ORANGES

Boost

For extra fiber, supplement with a teaspoon of ground flaxseeds.

Benefits

This combination helps break down and eliminate uric acid, making it an outstanding juice for people with acid conditions like rheumatism, gout, arthritis, and acne. Rich in iron and antioxidants, this juice also builds your blood, boosts your immune system, and protects your heart. Cherry juice is a top-notch remedy for constipation.

Cranberry Revival

You'll love drinking this tangy juice in the fall when cranberries and apples are fresh and abundant. This juice cleanses and rejuvenates your digestive and urinary tracts. It also helps your body eliminate toxins and protects it from disease.

½ CUP CRANBERRIES
1 CUP PURPLE OR RED GRAPES
  (SEEDS ARE FINE TO JUICE)
2 APPLES
½ LIME

Benefits

As natural diuretics, cranberries and grapes serve as effective medicine for the urinary tract. Both of these fruits can also be useful for treating kidney infections and stones. Rich with minerals and powerful antioxidants, this juice helps purify your blood, inhibit cancer and tumor growth, protect your heart, and stimulate metabolism.

Tip

When fresh or frozen cranberries are not available, I use soaked dried cranberries. Studies indicate that dried berries are just as nutritious as fresh ones, if not more so.

Summer Spritzer

This light, sparkling juice is as satisfying to your thirst as it is to the eye. Beautiful and perfect for weight watchers, this spritzer is rich in antioxidants that fight disease and rejuvenate your skin.

2 PEACHES
2 APRICOTS (OR 4 DRIED APRICOTS, SOAKED)
¼ CUP RASPBERRIES
½ CUP SPARKLING WATER (ADD AFTERWARD)

Benefits

These fruit juices work magic on your digestive tract, especially your colon. Both peaches and apricots help alleviate constipation and keep you regular. Their anti-aging properties also help reduce wrinkles. Apricots help tighten and tone your skin. Raspberries promote soft, smooth skin and help minimize acne. Apricots and raspberries are two of the most potent cancer-fighters in the fruit world. Rich in sulfur and vitamins A and E, they help prevent lung, stomach, and skin cancer as well as improve your eyesight.

Cucumber Cooler

This recipe always comes to mind in August when everyone in my family wants a drink that's energizing, thirst-quenching, and cooling. More than just a cool drink on a hot day, however, Cucumber Cooler is a natural diuretic that relieves water retention and promotes weight loss.

1 APPLE
1 CUP GREEN GRAPES
½ CUCUMBER

Boost

I sometimes add a teaspoon of apple cider vinegar.

Benefits

Apple and grape juices cleanse your arteries and colon, helping remove cholesterol and toxins. Cucumber and grape juices benefit the kidneys and urinary tract and can even help relieve bladder infections. Cucumber juice soothes all inflammations, including acne and ulcers. Externally applied, cucumber juice even cools sunburn and irritated, itchy eyes.

Warm Apple Cobbler

A cold-weather favorite, this warm drink often ends up in a thermos, packed along with mittens, scarves, and the toboggan. Because they improve circulation and generate heat in your body, ginger and cinnamon help keep you warm all day long.

2 APPLES
1-INCH PIECE OF FRESH GINGER
1 BANANA
3 DATES, SOAKED AND PITTED
1 PINCH PUMPKIN PIE SPICE OR CINNAMON
½ CUP WATER OR MILK

Juice the apple and ginger, then blend with the remaining ingredients. Pour into a saucepan and heat. If you like it tangy, add a squeeze of lemon juice.

Benefits

Well-known energizers like apple, date, and banana make this a good drink to start your day with. Dynamic spices like ginger and cinnamon stimulate your digestive fire and metabolism. This juice is also a tasty way to strengthen your immune system and keep yourself regular.

Sweet Sunburst

My friends are always delighted to learn that something that tastes this sensational is also good for their health. This luscious juice not only helps digestion but also beautifies your skin.

2 CUPS PAPAYA
2 ORANGES
5 STRAWBERRIES

Boost

Try adding a teaspoon of bee pollen. If you want more fiber, juice the oranges manually, then blend with the papaya and strawberries to make a smoothie rather than a juice.

Benefits

Besides cleansing and regulating your digestive tract, this fresh combination replenishes your body with energy and vital fluids. It also helps reduce acidity and alleviate rheumatoid pain. These cooling, strengthening fruits make a helpful tonic for the throat and lungs, helping relieve cough and congestion. They also help clear up skin conditions like acne, eczema, and psoriasis.

Peach Party

This juice can do wonders in creating a peaches and cream complexion. An effective cleanser for the digestive tract, this recipe can also help lower blood pressure and cholesterol.

3 PEACHES
1 APPLE
1 CUP PURPLE GRAPES

Benefits

Peaches have a tightening and toning effect on your skin, while all the fruits in this recipe cool the body and cleanse your intestines and arteries. Peaches can also help relieve inflammation, dry cough, and constipation.

Sweetie Pie

By introducing our children to juicing, we're leading them onto a path of lifelong health. Getting them started couldn't be easier than with this dessert-like recipe.

1½ CUPS RED OR PURPLE GRAPES
3 RED PLUMS
4 DATES, SOAKED AND PITTED

Boost

For extra fiber, supplement with a teaspoon of ground flaxseeds. Add fresh ginger for spice and energy.

Benefits

Not only does this juice cleanse your digestive tract, but it also helps unclog arteries. Grape juice in particular helps remove cholesterol from your arterial walls and heart, reducing the risk of a heart attack or stroke. Purple grape juice also guards against cancer and viruses. This recipe is an excellent source of energy.

Cherry Melon Blush

I wish cherries were in season year-round. In late summer I often make pitchers of this juice for my family and neighbors. Loaded with minerals, both cherry and watermelon juices flush poisons, acids, and waste from the body, making this combination ideal for arthritis sufferers. Watermelon juice is a first-rate kidney and bladder cleanser.

2 CUPS WATERMELON
12 PITTED CHERRIES
1-INCH PIECE OF FRESH GINGER

Benefits

High in iron, cherries build and detoxify your blood. They also protect your skin. Both cherries and watermelon flush acids from the body, especially uric acid. Watermelon is perhaps the best diuretic of all fruits, meaning it helps reduce water retention and helps weight loss. Juice the seeds as well if you want a more thorough effect (don't worry, it won't affect the taste of the juice). The lycopene in watermelon fights prostate cancer and premature aging. Cherries also benefit the prostate.

Tip

When cherries aren't in season, I either use frozen cherries or make this juice without them. Delicious on its own, watermelon-ginger juice is a combination I've often used for juice fasting.

Citrus Splendor

Packed with vitamin C and bioflavonoids, this lively citrus blend boosts your immune system and helps keep your skin looking radiant.

1 PINK OR RUBY RED GRAPEFRUIT
2 ORANGES
1 TANGERINE
¼ LEMON
¼ LIME

Boost

Enhance the antioxidant power of this juice with a dash of cayenne pepper.

Benefits

This juice combats colds, flus, and most other challenges to your immune system. Citrus is helpful for sore throats (even strep throat) and for clearing mucus from the lungs. It also strengthens blood vessels (especially if you include some of the nutrient-rich white pith).

Watermelon Wave

Perfect when lounging by the pool, this summer special works wonders in reducing water retention. Natural diuretics like melon and cranberry ease uncomfortable bloating and cleanse the kidneys of toxins. They simultaneously replenish fluids and refresh your palate.

2 CUPS WATERMELON
1 CUP PAPAYA
¼ CUP CRANBERRIES
(FRESH, FROZEN, OR SOAKED DRIED)

Boost
It never hurts to add some fresh ginger.

Benefits
Both watermelon and cranberries help flush uric acid from your body, relieving arthritis and gout, renewing the blood, and improving your skin. Because they help eliminate excess fluids from your body, these fruits are also great for weight loss. Cranberries cleanse the urinary tract and help treat bladder, kidney, and urinary tract infections.

Mango Milk

Simple yet scrumptious, this silky blend features the king of fruits, the luscious mango. According to Ayurveda, the combination of mango and milk restores health and strength and promotes longevity. I always find it amazing that just two ingredients can produce such an astounding taste.

Blend:

1 TO 2 CUPS MILK (ACCORDING TO DESIRED THICKNESS)
1½ CUPS MANGO
A FEW ROSE PETALS FOR GARNISHING

Benefits

The ancient practice of Ayurveda, which means "science of life," deems this recipe among the finest for rebuilding strength and relieving exhaustion. This recipe is perfect for those recovering from illness or injury. Milk improves your memory, while mango increases iron absorption and helps preserve eyesight.

Nectarine Dream

Each year I take full advantage of nectarine season by juicing them. Quality nectarines are generally found from mid-May until October. Though nothing beats fresh, in winter months I use soaked dried peaches or apricots instead of nectarines.

3 OR 4 NECTARINES
⅓ CUP BLUEBERRIES
2 APPLES

Benefits

Cooling nectarine juice soothes the colon, while the pectin in apples and blueberries cleanses and detoxifies it. Blueberries contain some of nature's most powerful antioxidants and help fight cancer, heart disease, and urinary tract infections. They may also help improve brain function and memory.

Asian Sensation

In this recipe, crisp, juicy Asian pears yield a sweet, delicate juice that's wonderful for quenching your thirst. When they're in season throughout June and July, fragrant lychees lend an exotic touch. The highest-quality lychees are nicely perfumed, with deep red skin and milky white flesh.

1 ASIAN PEAR
1½ CUPS PINEAPPLE
8 LYCHEES, PEELED AND PITTED (OPTIONAL)
¼ CUP COCONUT MILK (ADD AFTERWARD)

Benefits

High in vitamin C, this juice helps ward off flu, colds, and sore throats. According to Eastern medicines, it is also a nourishing combination for the lungs and may even be helpful for asthmatics.

Tip

This juice is particularly delicious on ice.

Blue Pineapple

Satisfying more than just your sweet tooth, this delicious summer juice also satisfies your body's need for enzymes and antioxidant protection.

1½ CUPS PINEAPPLE
¼ CUP BLUEBERRIES
1 APPLE

Boost

I like to add a teaspoon of bee pollen.

Benefits

Try this vitamin C–rich recipe instead of a citrus blend whenever you have a sore throat, a cold, or laryngitis. Bromelain, a powerful anti-inflammatory and antibacterial enzyme in pineapple, aids digestion and helps relieve pain. Phytochemicals in blueberries help maintain healthy eyes. Whenever possible, try to get wild blueberries.

Beauty Boost

Sometimes known as the "beauty fruit," apricots are rich in vitamins, minerals, enzymes, amino acids, and essential oil—all vital nutrients for keeping a clear, youthful complexion.

4 APRICOTS (OR 8 DRIED APRICOTS, SOAKED)
⅓ CUP BLACKBERRIES (FRESH OR FROZEN)
3 ORANGES

Boost

You can enhance the potency of this juice with a teaspoon of bee pollen.

Benefits

Concentrated with antioxidants like beta-carotene, lycopene, and vitamins C and E, this juice helps keep your skin and tissues flexible and healthy. Blackberries and apricots especially promote a clear, youthful complexion. More than just a beauty boost, however, these fruits also help prevent cancer, heart disease, and anemia.

Tip

If fresh apricots aren't in season, don't worry. Studies have shown that their dried counterparts are even more concentrated with nutrients, especially the carotenoid lycopene.

VEGETABLE JUICES

Nourish and rebuild your body on a cellular level.

Carotene Dream

Fresh kale and carrots are excellent sources of carotenoids like alpha- and beta-carotene, which convert to vitamin A once inside the body. Carotenoids work on a cellular level to prevent the formation of cancer and to slow the aging process.

6 CARROTS
3 KALE LEAVES
1 GREEN ONION

Boost

As in most juices, a little bit of fresh ginger is nice.

Benefits

This pungent combination is wonderful for your eyes, hair, teeth, bones, and complexion. A boost to your immune system, it can also help relieve cold and flu symptoms like lung congestion and fever. These vegetables are soothing to the stomach, especially kale, which can even reduce ulcer inflammation.

Greenhouse Special

Though this sweet, pungent juice serves your health in many ways, it is one of the best combinations for relieving constipation. Cabbage juice also helps restore friendly bacteria to your intestines.

1½ CUPS CABBAGE
1½ CUPS SPINACH
2 APPLES

Boost

Supplement with a teaspoon of apple cider vinegar.

Benefits

This juice soothes and stimulates your digestive tract. Apples contain pectin, a carbohydrate that forms a gel in your digestive tract. This gel absorbs and dissolves toxins and stimulates movement in the bowels. Spinach cleanses the digestive tract, while cabbage juice heals intestinal irritation. This recipe fights fatigue, wrinkles, and anemia and helps cleanse your liver and kidneys.

Quiet Thyme

If someone you care about suffers from asthma or a persistent cough, this is a pleasant combination you'll want to share because of its calming, disinfecting, and nourishing effect on the lungs. I have this juice at least once a week.

½ ORANGE SWEET POTATO
2 CARROTS
3 JERUSALEM ARTICHOKES (ABOUT 1 CUP)
1 HANDFUL SUNFLOWER SPROUTS
1 TSP. FRESH THYME

Benefits

Bursting with beta-carotene, vitamin C, and potassium, this mellowing, grounding recipe protects your heart, fights cancer, and helps preserve eyesight. Sweet potato and sunflower sprouts build chi, while sweet potato has long been considered a mood-lifting food. Thyme can help take the edge off menstrual cramps.

Liquid Sunshine

I love the creamy yet refreshing effect parsnips give to juices. Combined with peppery arugula and aromatic parsley, this cleansing juice is bursting not just with flavor, but also with chlorophyll, beta-carotene, and a wealth of minerals. It rejuvenates the digestive and urinary tracts and helps relieve constipation.

1 HANDFUL ARUGULA
3 APPLES
2 PARSNIPS
1 HANDFUL FRESH PARSLEY

Boost

I like to add a teaspoon of apple cider vinegar and/or green grass powder.

Benefits

This juice helps cleanse the blood, kidneys, liver, and intestines. It also stimulates organs like the spleen and gallbladder, which, according to traditional Chinese medicine, are both vital for digestion. Full of antioxidants, this juice benefits your heart and circulation and protects against cancer.

Power Cleanse

Everything we consume is processed by the liver before being assimilated into the body. Acting as a filter, the liver protects us from many of the harmful toxins present in today's food supply. This recipe reduces the risk of disease by helping the liver eliminate accumulated toxins, many of which could otherwise remain in the body for years.

2 LONG SPRIGS WATERCRESS
2 FRESH DANDELION LEAVES
1 BEET
2 CELERY STALKS
1 APPLE

Boost

Add a teaspoon of apple cider vinegar or a squeeze of lemon.

Benefits

Though most people think of dandelion as an annoying weed, it's really one of the most beneficial plants in nature, especially for the liver. This blend helps cleanse your liver, blood, and intestinal tract. It acts as a diuretic, increases bile production, and improves the function of your spleen, pancreas, and stomach. Full of antioxidants, this juice is an excellent anticancer tonic.

Mother Earth

On a hot summer day, this mellow, cooling juice is perfect to sip in the shade. Soothing to your stomach and satisfying to your palate, this is a wonderful tonic for relieving indigestion and ulcer inflammation. Garnish with your favorite fresh herb.

1 CUP FENNEL
½ CUCUMBER
2 KALE LEAVES
3 CARROTS

Boost

Add a 1-inch piece of fresh ginger.

Benefits

Cucumber and carrot juices have an alkalizing and therefore soothing effect on the digestive system, while kale juice helps relieve ulcer pain. Fennel helps ease an upset stomach, gas, and indigestion. If you frequently eat high-fat, heavily spiced foods, I recommend fennel juice to avoid heartburn and aid digestion.

Strength Builder

A favorite among the athletes in my family, this sweet, spicy tonic strengthens the chi, or life energy. It is rich in vitamins and minerals, especially vitamin A and calcium, which strengthen bones, teeth, skin, and muscles.

6 CARROTS
1 HEAPING HANDFUL SPINACH
2 LONG SPRIGS WATERCRESS
1 TSP. FRESH TARRAGON

Boost

For extra energy, add a teaspoon of green grass powder or an ounce of wheatgrass juice.

Benefits

The chlorophyll and iron in this juice help purify, oxygenate, and build blood. Both spinach and watercress juices act as diuretics, helping the body get rid of excess fluid and waste. Spinach juice is even an effective laxative.

Fat Burner

Many people have trouble keeping their weight down and balancing their blood sugar. Healthy and satisfying, this spicy refreshment curbs the appetite, stimulates metabolism, and helps regulate blood sugar levels. It is a blessing for diabetics and hypoglycemics.

2 CARROTS
2 CELERY STALKS
3 JERUSALEM ARTICHOKES (ABOUT 1 CUP)
1-INCH PIECE OF FRESH GINGER
1 PINCH GROUND MUSTARD
A SLIVER OF FRESH HOT CHILI PEPPER
(BIRD'S EYE, JALAPEÑO, OR WHATEVER YOU PREFER)

Benefits

Jerusalem artichokes, also called sunchokes, are high in inulin, a nondigestible carbohydrate that satisfies the body's cravings for things like bread and pasta without disrupting blood sugar levels. Hot chilies, ginger, and mustard stimulate the entire metabolic system. Hot chilies also contain the magic combination of copper and phosphorus, often thought to have a fat-burning chemistry.

Tip

The hottest part of a chili is just around the seeds. If your tolerance for heat is low, avoid this area entirely, using only the flesh further away from the seeds. Never touch your eyes right after handling hot chilies.

Red Refresher

Beets are nearly unbeatable for cleansing the body, especially in this sweet and spicy blend. Energizing and strengthening, this juice cleanses the digestive tract, liver, and blood. I like to drink it in the morning to get my circulation flowing.

½ RED BELL PEPPER
1 BEET
2 APPLES
1 HEAPING HANDFUL SPINACH
CAYENNE PEPPER TO TASTE

Benefits

Apple and beet are two of the best cleansers in the fruit and vegetable kingdom. The pectin in apple forms a gel in the intestines that absorbs and dissolves toxins and relieves constipation. Rich in iron and copper, this juice is also a powerful blood builder and purifier. According to Eastern medicines, red-colored juice improves circulation and strengthens the heart.

Vitality Juice

For years I've had fun asking friends to guess the ingredients of a drink they find delicious. The most fun is seeing their faces when they realize veggies like cabbage or radish are the main ingredients! Zesty, sweet, and slightly pungent, this unique, tasty juice helps normalize thyroid function and metabolism, making it a great recipe for weight loss.

2 RADISHES
1 HEAPING HANDFUL ALFALFA SPROUTS
1½ CUPS CABBAGE
1½ PEARS

Boost

Supplement with a teaspoon of green grass powder or an ounce of wheatgrass juice.

Benefits

If the thyroid is underproductive, the result can be weight gain and lethargy. If overproductive, the result can be weight loss and anxiousness. The thyroid regulates your metabolism, and radishes help regulate the thyroid. Alfalfa and cabbage also support the thyroid and serve as overall health tonics, strengtheners, and cleansers.

Sunny Energizer

This is a delicious new favorite of mine that's good any time of the day. Bursting with nutrients like omega-3 essential fatty acids, chlorophyll, and silicon, this juice is a general health tonic.

2 CARROTS
2 CELERY STALKS
1 APPLE
1 PINCH GROUND CUMIN
1 HEAPING HANDFUL SUNFLOWER
SPROUTS

Boost

Add a teaspoon of green grass powder or an ounce of wheatgrass juice.

Benefits

These combined ingredients help cleanse and soothe the gastrointestinal tract. They have a calming effect on the nervous system and help strengthen the gallbladder, liver, and circulatory and lymphatic systems. Silicon strengthens and tones all body tissues, including skin, arteries, and muscles.

Silky Green Bean Cocktail

A terrific recipe for people with blood sugar problems, this juice is refreshing, balancing, and nourishing.

5 JERUSALEM ARTICHOKES (ABOUT 1½ CUPS)
1 CUP GREEN BEANS
1 PEAR
1 TSP. LIME JUICE OR APPLE CIDER
   VINEGAR

Boost

To enhance the benefits of this juice, add a teaspoon of green grass powder and/or blend with 2 Tbsp. avocado.

Benefits

Jerusalem artichokes contain inulin, a nondigestible carbohydrate that satisfies cravings for carbohydrates without upsetting blood sugar levels. It also stimulates the production of insulin, rejuvenates the liver, and promotes the growth of friendly bacteria in the digestive tract. Rich in plant-based estrogen, green beans can benefit women experiencing PMS and menopause.

Fall Harvest

Fresh, sweet, and savory, this earthy autumn juice helps alkalize your body and restore balance. It can also ease heartburn and indigestion.

2 PARSLEY OR PARSNIP ROOTS
2 CARROTS
1 SWEET POTATO
1 TSP. FRESH DILL

Benefits

Combining some of nature's most alkalizing vegetables, this juice helps reduce high acidity in the body caused by eating too many acid-forming foods like sugar and meat. It also has a beautifying effect on your complexion, helping soothe conditions like acne, eczema, and psoriasis. A natural diuretic, this juice also helps rid the body of stored waste.

Tip

Sometimes sweet potato juice produces some fiber. If you find this undesirable, simply strain the juice before drinking.

Nature's Bounty

Providing an abundance of essential minerals that have been absorbed directly from the earth, this tasty root juice has for years been a popular source of strength and stamina in my family.

½ BEET
4 CARROTS
1 PARSNIP
1-INCH PIECE OF FRESH GINGER
3 LONG SPRIGS FRESH PARSLEY

Boost

Add a small clove of garlic or a dash of cayenne pepper.

Benefits

This juice strengthens your blood and circulation. It also cleanses your liver, kidneys, and digestive tract, helping prevent toxicity and disease, especially cancer. Carrots and parsnips help preserve your eyesight and reduce acid conditions like acne and arthritis. Root vegetables are by nature cleansing, grounding foods.

Asian Elixir

With juicy Asian pear and mineral-rich bok choy, this sweet, aromatic drink truly satisfies your thirst. It also strengthens your bones, teeth, and immune system.

3 LARGE BOK CHOY LEAVES
1 CUP BEAN SPROUTS
2 PARSNIPS
1 ASIAN PEAR
5 FRESH MINT LEAVES
1-INCH PIECE OF FRESH GINGER

Benefits

This calcium-rich juice strengthens your bones, hair, teeth, and nails. It can also be helpful if you suffer from arthritis, diabetes, high cholesterol, obesity, or fatigue. Mint and ginger are both mild stimulants, so you may not want to drink this combination before bed. Ginger improves digestion, metabolism, circulation, and immune function.

Tip

I always have this drink on ice.

Winter Revival

I've yet to find a better recipe to clear sinus congestion than this juice, a wintertime regular in my family. Don't go overboard on the horseradish, however; a little bit goes a long way.

½ RED POTATO
6 CARROTS
1 HEAPING HANDFUL FRESH PARSLEY
¼-INCH SLIVER OF HORSERADISH ROOT
(ABOUT THE SIZE OF A QUARTER) OR ½ TSP. PREPARED HORSERADISH

Boost

For extra fiber, add a teaspoon of ground flaxseeds.

Benefits

On cold days, horseradish warms you up while it cleanses the mucous membranes in your nasal passages and intestines. Potato juice can help your body eliminate toxic metal deposits like lead and mercury. Both parsley and carrot juices are excellent overall cleansers that promote digestion, detoxification, and rejuvenation.

Sweet Green Punch

This pleasant blend of vegetables and sweet apple helps purify the urinary tract and optimize kidney and liver function. An effective combination of natural diuretics, this juice is excellent for relieving fluid retention.

½ CUCUMBER
2 MEDIUM PARSNIPS
2 LONG SPRIGS WATERCRESS
1 HEAPING HANDFUL FRESH PARSLEY
1 APPLE

Boost

Add a teaspoon of apple cider vinegar.

Benefits

These vegetables, all natural diuretics, cleanse the bladder and kidneys, relieving edema. This combination also strengthens and purifies your digestive tract while providing a wealth of cancer- and tumor-fighting nutrients. Promoting weight loss, youthful skin, and fresh breath, this juice also builds your chi. Green juices calm and clarify your mind and rejuvenate your body.

Garden Dew

I don't often include garlic in my juice recipes, but this is a drink that wouldn't be complete without it. Rich in selenium, sulfur, and silicon, this nourishing combination actively fights free radicals and rejuvenates aging cells.

½ RED BELL PEPPER
2 CARROTS
2 CELERY STALKS
½ CUCUMBER
½ APPLE
½ CLOVE GARLIC

Benefits

Garden Dew nourishes and revitalizes your cells and works to improve the appearance of your skin from the inside out. The high potassium content helps tighten the collagen in your skin, while antioxidants fight wrinkles and other visible signs of aging. This juice also fights degenerative diseases like cancer, arthritis, and heart disease.

Summer Crush

Sometimes called the Mexican potato, jicama is a mildly sweet, crunchy vegetable that reminds me of a combination of apple and water chestnut. Naturally, I like to mix it with ginger. The result is a unique, refreshing juice that quenches thirst and invigorates the body.

1 CUP JICAMA
5 LETTUCE LEAVES (ROMAINE OR CURLY)
2 PEARS
1-INCH PIECE OF FRESH GINGER

Benefits

When drunk regularly, both jicama and lettuce juices can soothe varicose veins and hemorrhoids. Ginger is a vasodilator, meaning it dilates your blood vessels, improving circulation and helping remove cholesterol deposits. An effective remedy for constipation, nausea, and water retention, this juice also tastes delicious.

Tip

Jicama is sometimes gritty when juiced. If this happens, simply strain the juice before drinking. This recipe is also nice on ice.

Beauty Bouquet

Nothing more dramatically affects how our bodies will age than what we eat throughout our lives. Tight-skinned vegetables, for instance, contain properties that help keep your skin taut and glowing. The vegetables in this rich, tasty juice promote a creamy, toned, and youthful complexion.

½ CUCUMBER
2 CELERY STALKS
½ RED POTATO
2 CARROTS
6 PLUMP, PITTED OLIVES
A SQUEEZE OF FRESH LEMON JUICE

Benefits

The combination of silicon, selenium, beta-carotene, and potassium helps firm up collagen and give your skin a healthy glow. It also softens your skin and helps get rid of blemishes and redness around the nose. Olives not only beautify your skin, but regular consumption of them may even help prevent skin cancer.

Tip

Ideally, the olives should be raw and stored in water. If stored in oil, give them a good rinse before juicing them.

Sprout Sensation

My son was shocked to learn that his favorite green juice contained one of his least favorite vegetables, brussels sprouts. Truly refreshing, this blend tastes surprisingly good while it nourishes and protects your body against cancer and heart disease.

4 BRUSSELS SPROUTS
1 CUP JICAMA
⅓ GREEN BELL PEPPER
2 APPLES
½ CLOVE GARLIC

Benefits

Brussels sprouts and garlic are high in sulfur, which helps prevent cancer and tumor growth. Both garlic and apple juices help remove toxic metals like lead from the body. Garlic also fights everything from the common cold to viruses, harmful bacteria, intestinal parasites, and yeast infections.

Tip

Jicama can make this juice somewhat grainy. If this happens, simply strain before serving.

Sweet Clover

This zesty combination provides a burst of sprout energy, including a wealth of protein, vitamins, and iron. It also guards against cancer, tumors, and heart disease and helps purify your blood.

1 CUP CLOVER SPROUTS   1 CUP BROCCOLI
1 HANDFUL ARUGULA   3 APPLES

Boost

For extra energy and health protection, add an ounce of aloe vera juice and/or a teaspoon of green grass powder.

Benefits

Rich in chlorophyll, sulfur, protein, vitamins, minerals, enzymes, and plant-based estrogen, this juice is a superb source of nutrition. It helps lower cholesterol, relieve sore throats, and beautify your skin. Thanks to spicy clover and arugula, it can also stimulate your metabolism, improve circulation, and detoxify your blood and tissues.

Miss Scarlet

I always make this sweet, aromatic juice for my family during flu season. Packed with vitamin C and bioflavonoids, this recipe helps protect us from colds and viruses. It's also a top-notch cancer-fighter.

½ RED BELL PEPPER
3 TOMATOES
½ CUP CAULIFLOWER
½ BEET
3-4 SPRIGS FRESH CILANTRO

Boost

If you like your juice spicy, add a pinch of cayenne pepper for extra antioxidant protection.

Benefits

Aside from its flu-fighting abilities, this juice helps cleanse the liver, kidneys, and blood. In the process, your immune system is strengthened and its ability to fight disease is enhanced. Tomato, cauliflower, and beet are powerful warriors against cancer.

Restorative Elixir

When asparagus is in season, this is the first recipe to spring to mind. This delicious elixir helps release and eliminate toxins stored in your tissues. Cooling and alkalizing, it also helps reduce acidity in the body, relieve water retention, and prevent kidney stones.

2 MEDIUM TOMATOES
2 ASPARAGUS SPEARS
2 CARROTS
1 HANDFUL ALFALFA SPROUTS
1-INCH PIECE OF FRESH GINGER
A SLIVER OF LEMON (INCLUDING THE RIND)
A TWIST OF FRESH-GROUND PEPPER

Benefits

This healthy cocktail cleanses the kidneys, liver, gallbladder, and urinary tract. Tomatoes stimulate liver function, circulation, and digestion. Asparagus is one of the vegetable kingdom's most potent diuretics; it contains the unique alkaloid asparagine, which helps rid muscles and tissues of stored waste. Both asparagus and alfalfa make excellent tonics for juice fasting, detoxification, and weight loss.

Summer Glow

This sweet and slightly peppery juice is surprisingly delicious. Rich in silicon, chlorophyll, iron, and vitamins A and C, it also helps beautify your skin and hair and alleviate joint and muscle stiffness.

8 LARGE LETTUCE LEAVES (ROMAINE OR CURLY)
3 RADISHES
3 APPLES

Boost

Add a teaspoon of apple cider vinegar or an ounce of wheatgrass juice.

Benefits

Richer in silicon than most other garden vegetables, lettuce provides lubrication for your joints, combating rheumatism, arthritis, and gout. This recipe also stimulates digestion and clears your sinuses. Lettuce juice calms nerves and skin inflammations. Radish juice helps normalize thyroid function and metabolism.

Youth Juice

When people ask me how I have so much energy, I usually tell them it's because of juices like this one. Lively, light, and bursting with vital nutrients, this vegetable medley helps preserve youthful skin, improve metabolism, and protect your body from cancer.

2 RADISHES
½ CUP CAULIFLOWER
2 SPRIGS FRESH PARSLEY
2 CELERY STALKS
3 CARROTS

Boost

Enhance the potency of this juice with a small clove of garlic and/or a dash of cayenne pepper.

Benefits

This juice softens skin tissues and stimulates cell growth. Provitamin A (beta-carotene) regulates skin tone and protects against cell oxidation, a major cause of aging and disease. Youth Juice also boosts your immune system and helps prevent heart disease, eyesight degeneration, and cancer, especially breast cancer.

Tip

Buy radishes that still have their green tops. Radish greens wilt quickly, so if they're attached and in good form, it means the radishes are fresh. Radish greens are also nutritious and juiceable.

Beauty and the Beet

Historically underappreciated (people used to throw away the root and eat only the greens), the seemingly unimpressive beet root delivers impressive health benefits. Delicious beets help combat cancer and tumors, strengthen bones, reduce blood pressure, protect your heart, promote weight loss, and even beautify your skin.

1 BEET
½ CUCUMBER
3 ASPARAGUS SPEARS
1 APPLE

Boost

For extra nutrition, juice the beet greens as well.

Benefits

With effective diuretics like cucumber and asparagus, this juice also cleans the liver and urinary tract and can even help break up crystals and stones in the kidneys. I recommend this combination to friends who suffer from frequent bladder and urinary tract infections. This recipe also removes stored waste from your muscles and tissues and cleans your arteries.

Mineral Magic

The vegetables in this tasty recipe provide a mix of minerals that help alleviate symptoms of PMS like anxiety, irritability, mood swings, fatigue, and headache. Rich in calcium, this blend also helps prevent osteoporosis.

2 MEDIUM TOMATOES
3 CARROTS
1 PARSNIP
2 COLLARD GREEN LEAVES
1 SPRIG FRESH ROSEMARY (OPTIONAL)

Benefits

This beverage is particularly beneficial for the female body. It reinforces the immune system, strengthens your skeleton, and helps your body cope with stress. It's also good for regulating hormones and mood swings. Greens generally have a calming energy, while root vegetables like carrot and parsnip are grounding. Rosemary helps clear your head and relieve headaches.

Tip

For fun, I sometimes like to rim glasses with sea salt or celery salt. Just sprinkle some salt on a small plate, wet the rim of the glass with a slice of lemon or lime, then place the glass upside down into the salt and turn it a few times. When serving fruit juices, you can do the same thing, but with sugar.

Spicy Gazpacho

In another of nature's ironies, this spicy juice can be hot to the tongue but ultimately cooling to the body. It also supports thyroid and liver function, helping stimulate metabolism.

2 MEDIUM TOMATOES
½ CUCUMBER
1 CELERY STALK
2 RADISHES
1 GREEN ONION
2 LONG SPRIGS FRESH CILANTRO
A SLIVER OF FRESH HOT CHILI PEPPER

A SLICE OF LEMON AND PINCH OF BLACK PEPPER FOR GARNISHING

Benefits

Abundant in tomatoes, lycopene guards against certain forms of cancer, especially prostate cancer. Tomatoes also cleanse and tone your liver. Radish juice clears and soothes your nasal passages and digestive tract. Celery and cucumber have a soothing effect on the nervous system and skin. This is an excellent weight loss juice.

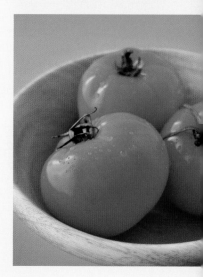

Tips

Spicy Gazpacho tastes fantastic with a bit of sweetness. Try blending the finished juice with a chunk of fresh mango. You can even rim the glass with sea salt or celery salt (see Tip on page 168). This juice is also nice on ice.

Evening Calm

In every culture, people like to end a hectic day with a soothing drink. Here's one that actually works and is good for you too. Mellow and delicious, this cooling juice helps calm your nervous system and curb your appetite.

½ CUCUMBER
2 CELERY STALKS
4 LETTUCE LEAVES
1 APPLE
4 FRESH BASIL LEAVES

Boost

To enhance the cooling nature of this juice, add a teaspoon of spirulina or an ounce of aloe vera juice.

Benefits

Naturally relaxing because of their color, green drinks are especially nice in the evening. This magnesium-rich potion calms your nerves and helps alleviate headache and nausea. It also possesses silicon, sulfur, and potassium, which help slow the aging process. Silicon is necessary for calcium metabolism and helps strengthen arteries, joints, and connective tissues.

Splendor in the Grass

Sometimes I come home and find my daughters wearing green masks. In fact, whenever they make this recipe, they always save some to put on their faces. Rejuvenating to more than just the complexion, however, this juice gives your entire body a welcome boost of energy.

1½ OZ. WHEATGRASS JUICE
1½ OZ. SPINACH JUICE

Benefits

This juice enlivens the appearance of your skin by tightening pores and replenishing elasticity. It also helps reduce conditions like acne and eczema. It helps treat anemia, relieve fatigue, regulate blood pressure, and neutralize cancer-causing carcinogens in the body. A wonderful tonic in general, it improves digestion and alleviates constipation.

Tip

If you don't like the taste, juice 2 apples or 2 cups pineapple to mix with the green juice.

How to Grow Wheatgrass at Home

If you can't find wheatgrass in your area or if you find it expensive, you can always grow it at home. Wheatgrass can even look beautiful growing in containers on your windowsill.

Necessary Supplies

TRAY(S) OR A SHALLOW BOX
SOIL
SEEDS
WATER

- Spread a 1-inch layer of fertile soil on a tray.

- Spread a thin layer of seeds across the soil and then cover with half an inch of soil.

- Wet the soil thoroughly, but don't overwater.

- Place the tray in the dark for 24 hours to let the seeds germinate.

- Put the tray by the window or underneath a grow light. Water in the mornings and evenings.

- Cut the grass when it's 5 to 7 inches high (approximately 5 to 7 days after germination).

- Once cut, the grass can grow for one or two more harvests.

SMOOTHIES

In our busy household, you'll hear the blender running
several times a day. Here's why.

Caribbean Dream

On hot, muggy days, this particular recipe is cooling and energizing. It also helps relieve water retention.

1½ CUPS PINEAPPLE (FRESH OR FROZEN)
JUICE OF 5 TANGERINES (OR 3 ORANGES)
1 CUP COCONUT MILK OR MILK
¼ CUP PISTACHIOS
1 SCOOP PROTEIN POWDER OR SPIRULINA

Benefits

A boost of vitamin C, enzymes, and protein, this recipe supports your immune and digestive systems. It also replenishes vital fluids and helps soothe sore throats, fevers, and arthritis.

Tip

Just as nutritious as oranges, tangerines can be a healthier alternative because they're usually sprayed with fewer pesticides.

Brownie Shake

My 6'2" son is about as comfortable in the kitchen as I would be in one of his martial arts tournaments. But give him a blender and a recipe like this one and he's the picture of self-sufficiency.

1 CUP MILK
1 TBSP. PEANUT BUTTER
1½ FROZEN BANANAS
1 SCOOP PROTEIN POWDER
1 TBSP. CAROB OR COCOA
    POWDER

½ CUP WATER
3 LARGE PITTED DATES
⅓ TSP. VANILLA
2 TBSP. CAROB OR
    CHOCOLATE CHIPS

Benefits

Perfect for athletes and growing kids, this smoothie is a great source of protein and energy.

Berry Explosion

I love going berry-picking in the summer. Not only is it fun, but it lets me provide my family with baskets full of these delicious disease-fighters. I always freeze batches of berries for the winter so we can make smoothies like this one all year round.

1 CUP FROZEN BERRIES OF CHOICE
1½ FROZEN BANANAS
1 CUP MILK
1 CUP WATER
2 TBSP. CASHEWS OR CASHEW BUTTER
2 TBSP. HONEY
1 SCOOP PROTEIN POWDER
½-INCH FRESH GINGER ROOT (OPTIONAL)

Benefits

Intensely colored and bursting with flavor, each berry is truly an explosion of nutrition. Richer in antioxidants than most other fruits, berries help do everything from prevent anemia, urinary tract infections, and eyesight degeneration to fight more serious conditions like heart disease, cancer, and stroke.

Silken Strawberry Whip

Moisturize your skin from the inside out. This light, creamy smoothie is a blessing for both your complexion and your taste buds.

1½ CUPS PAPAYA
6 STRAWBERRIES
1 GENEROUS TBSP. AVOCADO
1 TBSP. MAPLE SYRUP
⅓ CUP WATER OR MILK

Boost

Add a scoop of protein powder and this drink will keep you going for hours.

Benefits

Besides moisturizing, toning, and protecting your skin, these fruits are also excellent for lowering cholesterol and strengthening your blood. Natural oils from the rich avocado nourish your body and help conditions like eczema, dandruff, and stiff joints. Rich in lecithin, avocado also supports brain function and circulation. All of these fruits are great sources of potassium, which is sometimes known as the "youth mineral."

Mango Bananarama

I like to turn mango, my favorite fruit, into a more substantial breakfast by combining it with nuts and banana. Whenever I need to skip lunch, this is a breakfast that keeps me going until dinner.

1½ CUPS MANGO (FRESH OR FROZEN)
1 FROZEN BANANA
15 CASHEWS
1 TBSP. LIME JUICE
1 CUP MILK OR COCONUT MILK
1 SCOOP PROTEIN POWDER OR SPIRULINA
1 CUP WATER
1 TBSP. MAPLE SYRUP (OPTIONAL)

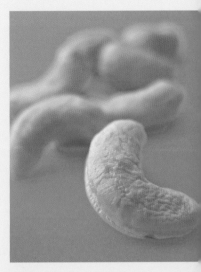

Benefits

Rich in potassium, beta-carotene, calcium, and protein, this recipe helps strengthen and protect your heart, bones, and teeth. Cashews are a very good source of magnesium, which is essential for calcium absorption.

Tip

In my travels, I have found that the best mangoes grow in India, the Philippines, and Hawaii. (Of course, some of my friends from Jamaica or Australia would want to argue with me about that.)

Sweet Relaxation

Some of my friends aren't sure what to think when they hear of recipes like this one, but when they try it, they're immediately won over. Adding herbs to juices and smoothies lends an exotic twist as well as extra healing powers. I'm particularly fond of basil, which makes this combination very relaxing for the mind and soothing for the stomach.

JUICE OF 2 APPLES
1½ FROZEN BANANAS
5 FRESH BASIL LEAVES
½ CUP MILK, COCONUT MILK, OR WATER

Benefits

This smoothie soothes and coats the stomach and digestive tract. To calm an upset stomach, blend in some apple pulp. Basil aids digestion and eases stomach cramps, nausea, and constipation.

Chai Hazelnut Smoothie

If you like the exotic spices of traditional chai tea, you'll love this delicious nutty shake. A meal in itself, this recipe provides sustenance for people who are physically active.

1 CUP MILK
¾ CUP CHAI TEA OR CHAI TEA MIX
2 TSP. FRESH GINGER JUICE
1½ FROZEN BANANAS
1 HEAPING TBSP. HAZELNUTS
1 OR 2 TBSP. MAPLE SYRUP, OR TO TASTE
1 PINCH CINNAMON
1 TSP. FLAX OIL
1 SCOOP PROTEIN POWDER

Benefits

Chai tea is full of digestive herbs like cinnamon, clove, and nutmeg. Combined with ginger, this smoothie is a perfect breakfast for jump-starting your digestion and circulation. It also provides antioxidants and essential fatty acids, which are helpful for lowering cholesterol, losing weight, and preventing disease. Hazelnuts are uniquely delicious and lower in fat than most other nuts.

Tip

Make ginger juice either with your juicer or simply by grating some fresh ginger and manually squeezing the pulp.

Mango Lassi

During mango season, this internationally famous fruit finds its way into my blender nearly every day. Simple and scrumptious, this classic Indian recipe works equally well as a drink or dessert.

1 CUP FROZEN MANGO
1 CUP VANILLA YOGURT
¾ CUP WATER
¼ TSP. ROSE WATER

Benefits

Mangoes help beautify your skin, protect against cancer, and support digestion because they are rich in beta-carotene and enzymes. Yogurt promotes the growth of friendly bacteria in the digestive tract, improving digestion and strengthening the immune system. Yogurt is an excellent source of calcium, protein, and vitamin B_{12}.

Tip

Vary the consistency of a lassi by reducing or adding water.

DESSERTS

Being healthy doesn't mean cutting out dessert,
it means getting creative.

DESSERTS

Almost everyone likes dessert. That little bit of sweetness somehow seems necessary after a savory meal. If you are lucky enough to have a Champion or other similar juicer, you'll notice you can make a variety of desserts like ice cream, sorbet, pudding, and pie filling. This is made possible by a piece of equipment called a blank. The blank is inserted in place of the filter. Rather than separating the juice from the pulp, the blank blocks the juice from coming out so that it gets pulverized with the pulp. Whatever food you put through your juicer—whether it's fresh or frozen fruits, frozen yogurt, nuts, or seeds—will come out blended to an ideal consistency when the blank is installed.

So rather than ruining a healthy meal with an unhealthy dessert, try the following nutritious recipes. I guarantee you'll find them as easy to make as they are delicious.

Rose Magic

This gorgeous dessert is my vegetarian version of Jell-O. Layers of fresh citrus, mango, and strawberry with rose essence create a luscious and healthy alternative to commercial gelatin-based desserts. You can vary the fruit to your liking, and don't worry, this recipe isn't nearly as complicated as it looks.

Layer 1

1 CUP TANGERINE JUICE
1 TBSP. GRANULATED FRUCTOSE
½ TSP. AGAR POWDER

Bring this mixture to a boil until the agar dissolves, about a minute. Pour it into a medium glass bowl. Freeze for 5 to 10 minutes to accelerate the gelling process.

Layer 2

1½ CUPS MANGO CHUNKS

Spread the mango chunks evenly over the first layer.

Layer 3

¼ CUP LEMON JUICE
¾ CUP WATER
3 TBSP. GRANULATED FRUCTOSE
1½ TBSP. RAW SUGAR
1 TSP. AGAR POWDER

Boil for a minute, or until the agar dissolves. Let the mixture cool slightly, then pour it over the mango layer. Freeze for 5 to 10 minutes while you prepare the next layer.

Layer 4

1 CUP STRAWBERRY SLICES

Spread the strawberry slices evenly over the previous layer.

Layer 5

1 TBSP. + 1 TSP. ROSE WATER
1 CUP WATER
1½ TBSP. RAW SUGAR
½ TSP. AGAR POWDER
¼ TSP. BEET POWDER

Bring the first 4 ingredients to a boil, then add the beet powder. Let the mixture cool, then pour it over the strawberries. Freeze for 10 minutes while you prepare the garnish.

Garnish

½ CUP MANGO, CHOPPED
½ CUP STRAWBERRY SLICES

Spread the mango and strawberries evenly over the top of the dessert. Chill for 1 to 2 hours before serving.

Serves 6-8

Mousse Royale

Although you may have heard that carob is no substitute for chocolate, here's a recipe that will satisfy even the most stubborn chocoholic. With only a small fraction of the fat and no caffeine, carob is far healthier and just as tasty as chocolate. My family even likes it better.

¾ CUP TOASTED ALMONDS (OR ½ CUP ALMOND BUTTER)
¼ CUP MAPLE SYRUP
½ TSP. VANILLA
2 TBSP. CAROB POWDER
1½ CUPS PLAIN LOW-FAT YOGURT
6 FROZEN BANANAS
⅓ CUP CAROB CHIPS
EXTRA CHIPS AND ALMONDS FOR GARNISHING

Mix the first 4 ingredients into the yogurt. Freeze the yogurt mixture for 3 hours so that it's firm but not frozen solid. Insert the blank and rotate pieces of banana and spoonfuls of the yogurt mixture through the juicer. Stir the chips into the mousse. Garnish and serve.

Serves 6-8

Cherry Vanilla Cream

My kids have never complained about my focus on nutrition because of amazingly delicious desserts like this one. High in flavor, low in fat, and completely satisfying, this five-minute recipe is sure to please all the ice cream lovers in your family.

2½ CUPS FROZEN CHERRIES
½ CUP HAZELNUTS
2 TBSP. RAW SUGAR
½ TSP. VANILLA
2 FROZEN BANANAS
WHIPPED CREAM
FRESH CHERRIES FOR GARNISHING

Mix the frozen cherries with the hazelnuts, sugar, and vanilla. Insert the blank and alternate the cherry-nut combination and banana through your juicer. Top with whipped cream and a cherry.

Serves 4

Berry Yogurt Delight

Though it has only three ingredients, this simple recipe tastes like you spent hours on it. Very luscious and easy to make, it has been a staple dessert in my family for over a decade.

2 CUPS FROZEN STRAWBERRIES
2 CUPS LOW-FAT STRAWBERRY YOGURT
½ CUP RAW SUGAR OR MAPLE SYRUP

Freeze the strawberries and yogurt the night before preparation. Remove them from the freezer about 15 minutes before use. Roll the strawberries in the sugar or maple syrup and cut the yogurt into chunks to fit your juicer. Install the blank and alternate the yogurt and coated strawberries through your juicer. Serve immediately.

Tip

You don't want to freeze this dessert (or similar recipes) for more than a couple of hours because it will solidify and lose its soft, creamy texture.

Serves 4

Pineapple Cashew Mousse

This silky, sweet dessert includes cardamom, one of my favorite Indian spices. Used just as often in sweet as in savory recipes, cardamom makes a wise addition to any dessert because of its digestive properties. In fact, traditional Indian restaurants typically serve cardamom after meals to aid digestion and sweeten the breath.

⅓ CUP CASHEWS
¼ CUP MAPLE SYRUP
1 TSP. CARDAMOM PODS OR PIECES
3 CUPS FROZEN PINEAPPLE CHUNKS
1½ CUPS FROZEN SILKEN TOFU CHUNKS
WHOLE CASHEWS AND FRESH PINEAPPLE FOR GARNISHING

Place the cashews, maple syrup, and cardamom in a cup. Insert the blank and alternate the nut mixture, pineapple, and tofu through the juicer. Stir the mousse, then freeze for 15 minutes. Garnish with whole cashews and slices of fresh pineapple.

Serves 6

Mango Pudding

Two blocks from our house, there's a local fruit stand that sells the most luscious mangoes I've ever tasted. From late May to September—a time my daughters refer to as Mango-Fest—we buy them nearly every day to make this dreamy pudding for dessert.

3 CUPS FROZEN MANGO
2 FROZEN BANANAS
½ CUP PITTED DATES
1 CUP FROZEN COCONUT MILK
FRESH MANGO OR BANANA SLICES FOR GARNISHING

Insert the blank and rotate the ingredients through your juicer. Freeze for 15 minutes. Garnish with fresh mango or banana slices.

Serves 6

Maple Ginger Applesauce

Traditional applesauce stews for hours on the stovetop, cooking the nutrients away. I'd rather serve applesauce cool and fresh, with all the nutrients still intact. With just the right amount of spice, tang, and sweetness, this easy yet nutritious recipe satisfies cravings for dessert without adding loads of fat or calories.

4 APPLES
2 PEARS
2 TBSP. FRESH GINGER JUICE
1 TBSP. FLAX OIL
2 TBSP. MAPLE SYRUP
2 TBSP. LEMON JUICE
2 TBSP. TOASTED SESAME SEEDS
½ TSP. CINNAMON (OR PUMPKIN PIE SPICE)

Insert the blank and rotate pieces of apple and pear through the juicer. Stir in the remaining ingredients and serve chilled or at room temperature.

Tip

You can make fresh ginger juice either with your juicer or simply by grating fresh ginger, then squeezing the pulp manually.

Serves 4-6

Rainbow Popsicles

The only ingredient needed for this recipe is your favorite fruit. Mango, papaya, pineapple, and melon tend to work best because their pulp has a pleasant consistency. I keep these popsicles in the freezer all the time, and not just for the kids.

You will need:

- POPSICLE MAKERS (FOUND AT MOST MAJOR GROCERY STORES)
- A JUICER OR BLENDER
- YOUR FAVORITE FRUIT

Insert the blank and pass 2 or 3 cups of melon, mango, papaya, or whatever fruit you like through the juicer. Pour the puree into popsicle makers and freeze. You can also make these popsicles from fresh juices.

PULP POSSIBILITIES

Nothing goes to waste in my kitchen.

Pulp Possibilities

Soups

Vegetable pulp still contains valuable flavors and nutrients that are perfect for texturizing soups.

Sauces

Adding veggie pulp to homemade tomato sauce gives it a texture similar to ground beef—only it cleanses your arteries rather than clogs them. It's also a healthier alternative to textured vegetable protein (TVP).

Salads

A few tablespoons of carrot or beet pulp can make a light salad seem more substantial. Throw together some greens, tomatoes, cucumber, olives, and pulp, top it with your favorite dressing, and you have yourself a light, nutritious meal. Veggie pulp is also a wonderful addition to coleslaw.

Sandwiches

Add some seasoned salt and lemon juice to veggie pulp and sprinkle it in your favorite sandwich.

Breads and Baked Goods

Fruit and vegetable pulps can bring flavor and fiber to all kinds of breads, muffins, and cakes.

Salsa

Tomato and red bell pepper pulp make the perfect addition to fresh homemade salsa. Try adding a couple spoonfuls of pineapple pulp as well.

Veggie Paté

Pick your favorite fresh herbs, nuts, seeds, and spices and create your own unique veggie spread. Put it on crackers or celery or in sandwiches to make healthy snacks and lunches.

Vegetarian Burgers and No-Meatballs

It's easy to make rich, flavorful meat substitutes by mixing leftover vegetable pulp with seeds, onions, garlic, tofu, and whole wheat flour. They make wonderful transitional dishes for people moving toward a healthy vegetarian diet.

Three Different Pulp Patés

Just like with these recipes, I sometimes come up with the best combinations when I'm low on groceries and have only a small selection of ingredients. Now I make these dishes regularly no matter how well-stocked my cupboards are. Filled with fresh herbs, toasted nuts, and loads of fiber, these three vegetable patés are perfect for healthy sandwiches, dips, and spreads.

Toasted Sunflower Paté

Nutty and fresh with a dash of spicy mustard, this aromatic paté is great on crackers or toast.

2 CUPS CARROT-BEET PULP (OR SIMILAR)
⅓ CUP TOASTED SUNFLOWER SEEDS
¼ CUP TOASTED ALMOND PIECES
2 CELERY STALKS, FINELY CHOPPED
3 GREEN ONIONS, FINELY CHOPPED
½ CUP FRESH BASIL, HAND-TORN
2 TBSP. RICE VINEGAR
3 TBSP. OLIVE OIL
1 TSP. GROUND MUSTARD
2 TBSP. BRAGG LIQUID AMINOS
1 TSP. GROUND CORIANDER

Sesame-Mint Paté

Refreshing and tangy with little bursts of sweetness, this paté is perfect for filling celery stalks or pita bread.

2 CUPS CARROT-BEET PULP (OR SIMILAR)
¼ CUP TOASTED SESAME SEEDS
½ CUP FRESH MINT, CHOPPED
½ CUP CUCUMBER, PEELED, SEEDED, AND CHOPPED
2 RADISHES, FINELY CHOPPED
¼ CUP CURRANTS
¼ CUP BALSAMIC VINEGAR
3 TBSP. OLIVE OIL
1 TSP. SALT
1 TBSP. NUTRITIONAL YEAST

Fresh Herb and Feta Paté

This deliciously pungent paté is excellent for filling sandwiches and stuffing pastries.

2 CUPS CARROT-BEET PULP (OR SIMILAR)
2 CLOVES GARLIC, MINCED
2 TBSP. MILD MISO
½ CUP FETA CHEESE
⅓ CUP ROASTED CASHEW PIECES
⅓ CUP LEMON JUICE
1 TBSP. FRESH THYME
1 TBSP. FRESH ROSEMARY, CHOPPED
¼ CUP FRESH PARSLEY, CHOPPED
2 TBSP. OLIVE OIL

Veggie Hazelnut Burgers

Full of protein, fiber, and flavor, these burgers are delicious enough to encourage anyone to become vegetarian. My kids have been eating these since they were little. Serve them in wholegrain bread rolls with clover sprouts, ketchup, and your favorite mustard.

Burger mix

1½ CUPS CARROT-BEET PULP (OR SIMILAR)
1½ CUPS FIRM TOFU, CRUMBLED
¼ CUP SESAME SEEDS
¼ CUP NUTRITIONAL YEAST
⅓ CUP HAZELNUTS, CHOPPED
½ ONION, FINELY CHOPPED
3 TBSP. YOUR FAVORITE FRESH HERBS
1 CLOVE GARLIC
1 TBSP. FRESH GINGER, MINCED
2 TBSP. RAISINS, CHOPPED
2 TBSP. LIME JUICE
1 TSP. SALT
2 TBSP. OLIVE OIL
½ TSP. CAYENNE PEPPER (OPTIONAL)

Breading

½ CUP WHOLE WHEAT FLOUR
⅓ CUP SESAME SEEDS
2 TBSP. NUTRITIONAL YEAST
1 PINCH SALT

Mix all the burger ingredients together and form into patties. Dip each patty in the breading mixture until lightly coated. In a nonstick skillet, pan-fry the patties on medium heat in vegetable oil until golden brown, about 15 to 20 minutes. Makes 4 to 6 patties.

Pineapple Carrot Muffins

Sweet, tropical pineapple pulp makes a fine addition to sweets and pastries. Moist, fluffy, and full of fiber, this recipe has long been a brunch favorite in our home.

Preheat the oven to 350°F.

1 CUP PINEAPPLE PULP
½ CUP PINEAPPLE JUICE
1½ CUPS CARROT PULP
½ CUP APPLE JUICE
¾ CUP VEGETABLE OIL
½ CUP RAISINS
½ CUP WALNUTS OR PECANS, CHOPPED
1 CUP RAW SUGAR
1½ TBSP. EGG REPLACER POWDER
MIXED WITH ⅓ CUP WATER

2¾ CUPS WHOLE WHEAT PASTRY FLOUR
½ TSP. SALT
2 TSP. BAKING SODA
1½ TSP. BAKING POWDER
2 TSP. CINNAMON
1 TSP. GROUND GINGER
½ TSP. NUTMEG
¼ TSP. GROUND CLOVES

Mix each set of ingredients separately, then mix both together until well combined. Fill oiled muffin tins about 2/3 full. Bake for approximately 20 minutes.

Makes 2 dozen muffins

INDEX

With Appreciation to Champion

I would like to express my appreciation to the manufacturers of the Champion Juicer for helping make this book possible. For over half a century, the Champion family has made a high-quality juicer that is durable, powerful, versatile, and easy to use.

If you're interested in learning more about the simple and long-lasting Champion Juicer, visit the Champion website at www.championjuicer.com or email any questions to sales@championjuicer.com.

If you would like to purchase a new Champion 2000+ Juicer, you can order direct from Wai Lana and receive a 10% discount off the regular retail price.

Call 1-800-228-5145 to arrange payment and delivery.